Action
Tools for
Effective
Managers

Action Tools for Effective Managers

A Guide for Solving Day-to-Day Problems on the Job

Margaret Mary Gootnick
& David Gootnick

AMACOM
American Management Association
New York • Atlanta • Boston • Chicago • Kansas City • San Francisco • Washington, D.C.
Brussels • Mexico City • Tokyo • Toronto

This publication is designed to provide accurate and authoritative information in regard to the subject matter covered. It is sold with the understanding that the publisher is not engaged in rendering legal, accounting, or other professional service. If legal advice or other expert assistance is required, the services of a competent professional person should be sought.

Library of Congress Cataloging-in-Publication Data

Gootnick, Margaret Mary.
    Action tools for effective managers : a guide for solving day-to-day problems on the job / Margaret Mary Gootnick & David Gootnick.
        p.   cm.
    Includes index.
    ISBN 0-8144-7029-7
    1. Industrial management—Handbooks, manuals, etc.   2. Personnel management—Handbooks, manuals, etc.   I. Gootnick, David.
    II. Title.
    HD31.G595   1999
    658—dc21   99–31725
                                                                         CIP

Portions of this book appeared in somewhat different form in Action Tools for Successful Management by Margaret Mary Gootnick (Kendall Hunt Publishing Company, 1990).

Printing number

10   9   8   7   6

This book is lovingly dedicated to our beloved aunts, **Sr. Constance Marie** and **Sr. Ann Cletus** of The Sisters of Saint Joseph.

These wonderful and noble sisters have selflessly devoted their lives to helping others. And, in their deep faith and dedication, they have blessed so many with their gifts of love, caring, and compassion.

Contents

Section III
Team-Building Responsibilities   **55**

Section IV
Communicating for Positive Results   **73**

Section IX
Time and Stress Management   215

Preface

You've got a real management problem and need help now! The pressures of work build, and the problems facing you pile up. You don't have the luxury of time to contemplate theories or fads.

What you need are proven solutions and workable management tools. What's more, you deserve the best management advice possible.

Based on our nearly thirty years as management consultants to leading companies and trainers of tens of thousands of professional managers, we have identified sixty-eight of the most pressing—yet manageable—problems confronting today's working managers.

Action Tools for Effective Managers provides you with hundreds of ready-to-use management action tools for solving these important management problems and improving your group's productivity, quality, relationships, and results. Each chapter concisely describes a "real life" management case problem accompanied by a consultant's analysis and recommended management action tools.

We recommend use of the book as a troubleshooter's guide and daily reference manual for the active manager. As you experience a management problem at work, review the table of contents for the appropriate subject. Then find the chapter title and case problem closest to your situation. You can also examine the subject index at the back of the book for additional reference.

Action Tools for Effective Managers is a powerful problem-solving guide for individual managers. It also serves as a case book for stimulating discussion at management meetings, workshops, and courses.

We are grateful to Hank Kennedy, publisher of AMACOM Books, and Adrienne Hickey, executive editor of AMACOM Books, for their vision and interest in this book. In addition, we greatly appreciate Adrienne Hickey's keen insights, helpful feedback, and professional guidance throughout the book's development.

—Margaret Mary Gootnick and David Gootnick

Section I

Planning, Delegating, and Managing for Performance Success

1

Participative Action Planning

Case Problem: "Failing to Plan"

Two months ago, after joining the company as plant manager, Jim commissioned an employee feedback survey. Its purpose was to gather the feelings of the plant's workforce regarding the effectiveness of management.

Now, as Jim reads through the final survey report, he is bothered by several of the employees' comments:

"Planning . . . that's a laugh! I've never even seen a project plan. If there is one, the boss sure keeps it to himself."

"I don't think we operate according to well–thought-out plans. Just the other day, I asked my supervisor why we were using a particular type of grinding process. She said she didn't know, but it's always been done that way."

"We are always delivering our machines to customers in a rush situation, with many operating components not properly installed and customers returning at least 10 percent of the units as being totally unacceptable. The problem is that I know what's causing this situation: incorrect assembly methods, poorly trained workers, and salespeople making promises to customers without consulting our department for real-time scheduling capabilities. And what's worse is that our boss tells me to keep my ideas to myself and to follow the work plan that he has decided upon by himself."

"I don't sense that management really cares to tap its people's knowledge and expertise. The plans that managers make around here are so arbitrary and out of touch with reality! I've been around here for ten years, am considered a senior engineer by my peers, and have never once been asked by our managers to contribute my thoughts to project plans. Our managers think they know it all."

"I'll tell you why so many of our projects fail—it's because our supervisors constantly push for results but forget to invest any intelligent time on the planning side. Half of the time we don't know what the heck we're doing or why we're doing it."

"In our department, we plan to fail by failing to plan!"

Case Analysis

Jim has just been confronted with some important information that requires immediate attention. From his experience as a participative manager, Jim knows that these types of comments from employees suggest a plant-wide failure to make effective planning a top management priority in the conduct of business.

As a result, he decides to hold a staff meeting about the employee survey results, and to place at the top of the agenda the importance of effective planning and the process of participative action planning. He decides to open this meeting by quoting one of the comments given on the survey report: "We plan to fail by failing to plan!"

Action Tools

Planning is the necessary first step to launching and executing any successful job or project. Moreover, planning that optimally involves interested and knowledgeable employees in the process produces the very best results.

To effectively plan your department's work, consider the following action tools:

 Form a participative action planning team of individuals who could contribute valuable knowledge to the effort and would want it to succeed. This team would include individuals who might be assigned the work and those who have done similar work in the past, as well as customers who would receive outputs and benefits from the work team and suppliers who would provide key inputs and resources.

✱ As a team, flesh out the answers to the following six planning questions:

1. What are we trying to achieve?
2. Why is this important?
3. Who will participate in its undertaking?
4. How will the effort proceed?
5. Where will the various phases of the undertaking occur?
6. When will the final phase, as well as the intermediary phases, be completed?

✱ Prepare a written document that includes the answers to these questions and provides sufficient detail for taking necessary action. This written plan is both an energizing document, providing forward thrust to an important undertaking, and a stabilizing document, providing guidelines and checkpoints to assure successful completion.

✱ Give a copy of the plan to each individual involved in the project or job. This will provide a constant reminder of the "big picture" and the "road to travel" in completing this important work.

2

Performance Management

Case Problem: "The Cat and Mouse Game"

"Look Max, I don't really care anymore. You can talk all you want, but there's one thing I am sure of: Abe doesn't give a hoot about you or me or any other person in the accounting department. You're a fool to think otherwise."

"Calm down, calm down," Max advised his friend, Ken, who had just come out of his first performance review with their boss, Abe.

"Max, he put down everything—everything I've done over the year," claimed Ken. "He told me I had a lot of shaping up to do around here, and he pulled out a laundry list and mowed me down with charges of below-standard performance. Not once during the year did he say he was dissatisfied with my work or that he was going to write me up. From what he said in that meeting, you'd think I was a real zero! Max, I know my job inside and out, and I'm good at what I do."

"Did you say anything to him?" asked Max.

"What do you say to a person who rips you apart when you are expecting some pats on the back for a good year?" replied Ken. As the two men spoke, Abe, the accounting manager, passed their door and thought, "Just what I expected—those two guys loafing around when there's so much work to be done. And to think I set Ken straight in our meeting. I guess I'll have to straighten Max out, too. In fact, maybe I'll call him in my office in an hour and give him his performance review. It's about time for him, anyway. How I hate these things, but the boss says I've got to do it."

Case Analysis

On occasion, Abe spots errors and poor performance in his department but fails to bring these observations to the attention of his staff. Instead, he secretly logs them in private employee fact files, then presents these negative facts for the first time during performance review meetings.

What might be handled effectively on the spot when errors occur becomes a case of "I got ya!" The performance management process is not supposed to be a "cat and mouse" game, but rather a process of honest communication and continual performance improvement.

Ken, whose performance record is actually very good, is cast into a state of frustration by his manager's secretive approach. On the one hand, Ken has a very positive self-image. Yet, during the performance review meeting—an extremely important career event—his manager has succeeded in shocking, intimidating, and devaluing a competent and loyal professional accountant.

What has occurred here is more than a poor management practice; it is the creation of a threatening and negative climate that is highly destructive to departmental productivity.

Action Tools

Performance management is a vital process for enhancing performance and fostering a culture of continuous learning and development. It consists of three phases:

1. Performance planning
2. Performance feedback and coaching
3. Performance summary and development

To effectively manage employee performance in your department, consider the following action tools:

✦ Meet with each employee at the beginning of the year, and together create a written performance plan, spelling out clear expectations and performance standards for the coming year's work.

In each plan, include any new goals given to you by management that must be implemented across your department as well as any performance deficiencies that must be rectified by the individual. Have each individual sign the performance plan and retain a copy as a guide to the coming year's performance.

* Observe employee behavior and provide ongoing feedback and coaching, as necessary, for performance improvement. When you see your people doing good work, tell them so. If there's room for improvement, let them know.

* Maintain performance records, as appropriate, in employee fact files as well as commendations, complaints, and observations of very good or very poor performance as it relates to production, quality, safety, attendance, and teamwork.

* At least once a year, prepare a written performance summary and conduct a performance development meeting for each employee. In your summary, describe results achieved versus results expected, and point out any deficiencies requiring correction. In addition, ask employees to prepare their own written summary reports and bring them to their development meetings.

* During each performance development meeting, discuss your carefully prepared written summary, pointing out both strengths and deficiencies. Listen to the employee's viewpoint, and be prepared to modify your own report if new and compelling information is presented during the meeting. Conclude your meeting on a note of mutual agreement, and have the employee sign a copy of the agreed-upon written summary.

3

Resource Management

Case Problem: "The Means to an End"

"I'm stretched to the breaking point!" cried Tim, an associate buyer, to his colleague, Jeff. "Everything is ASAP and needed yesterday! All the projects I get from Irene, our dear purchasing manager, have unrealistically short deadlines. How about you . . . what's your situation?"

"I'm in the same boat as you, Tim," commiserated Jeff. "We never seem to have enough time to complete our work around here. But maybe with some more staff support, we could begin to see the light. You know, we have no real staff support and have to do every clerical job ourselves."

"Listen, who needs more clerks like Craig, who not only flirts with every passing female but can't type or file to save his life," replied Tim.

"You know, you're right," agreed Jeff. "Maybe we both should speak to Irene about our job needs. What were they again? More realistic deadlines, more staff support, and better-trained people."

"And let's not forget some basic tools and equipment for doing our work," added Tim. "The fact is that we need our own copy machine in purchasing. Whenever I need copies, the central office copier is always backlogged."

"That's funny you mentioned equipment," mused Jeff. "Did you know that for the last year I've been using my own laptop in the office service department to do my work?"

"No, I didn't," responded Tim. "That's ridiculous! These are basic tools; we need them. And we also need a water cooler that works."

"OK, OK, Tim," interrupted Jeff. "I think our request list is long enough. Let's not overtax Irene with too much responsibility. The fact is the things we're going to ask for should have been provided by her in the first place. It's her department, and all we want are the means to do our jobs well."

Case Analysis

From this dialogue, we can see that Irene, manager of corporate purchasing, is not properly planning for the resources needed to run her department. She is not acting as a "resource manager"— one who understands that results (output) depend upon sufficient resources (input).

Resource planning must be done at the beginning of each year as well as at the beginning of each assignment. The purchasing department, in this case, was underresourced in essential areas, thereby creating frustration and poor results for all.

The purchasing manager, in her resource management capacity, had the power to set her people up to succeed through the provision of proper supports, but instead, she set her people up to fail by not providing such supports.

Action Tools

A manager must understand the concept of resource management for smooth and efficient operations. As a resource manager, the manager sets his or her people up to succeed by providing proper resource support in each of these seven areas:

* *Money.* The department budget should cover all anticipated expenses within the fiscal year.
* *Staff.* Departmental staff should be appropriate in size to handle the magnitude of work assigned. In addition, personnel should be properly trained in all necessary skills.
* *Tools and equipment.* The physical tools and equipment of departmental operations as well as the physical facility must be maintained in good working order to allow departmental tasks to be completed as efficiently as possible.

✦ *Material.* Inventory of materials required in the department should be maintained.

✦ *Methods and procedures.* Each member of the department should have a clear job description, clearly defined goals for each task assigned, and access to current operating procedures.

✦ *Schedules.* Deadlines should be realistic and set in accordance with the staff's size and ability to accomplish work goals.

✦ *Information.* Information necessary for the accomplishment of assigned jobs must be provided to each member of the department. Such information could include changes in plans, policies, and procedures pertaining to the conduct of the department as well as management feedback on the performance of staff members and customer feedback on departmental effectiveness.

4

Delegating Job Assignments

Case Problem: "I Did It My Way"

"I can't take it anymore. I want out!" Mack cried in frustration to his boss, Jim, eastern regional sales manager.

"Hold on a minute!" said Jim. "You can't quit now. It's only been three months since your promotion to assistant eastern regional sales manager."

"Look, it's just not working out," said Mack.

"Let me remind you," Jim insisted, "that when you accepted the promotion three months ago, you flatly refused my offer for management training and my attempt to show you the ropes. You said you didn't need management training and that you could run this office with your eyes closed. So what do you do when you find out you're wrong and do need some help? Instead of coming to me, you act like a coward and want out without giving it a fair chance!"

"Everything you say is true," Mack admitted. "I really thought I'd be able to cut it as assistant regional manager on my own. Maybe I am giving up too easily. If you'd be willing to work with me now, I'd give it another shot."

"Agreed," replied Jim. "Now, tell me, what are your greatest frustrations?"

"First of all," Mack said, "as a sales rep, I used to have a personal life with time for relaxation and recreation. But now, as assistant manager, I'm always taking work home, and I frequently work late in the office just to stay afloat. And whenever I'm away from the office, papers pile up on my desk and nothing ever seems to get done. But the thing that really bugs me is that everyone here complains about having insufficient authority to make decisions."

"Why do you think your people would complain about having no authority?" asked Jim.

"Well, I'm the boss and it's my job to make the decisions," Mack replied. "Also, if someone messes up, I'm the one who gets blamed."

Case Analysis

Based upon Mack's description, Jim should be able to see a pattern emerging. In the eyes of the experienced manager, this pattern points strongly to one clear deficiency in our new assistant manager: ineffective delegation skills.

Because of his former "Do-the-Work-Yourself" orientation, Mack gets bogged down in doing everything himself. He has not yet realized the value of placing trust in employees and delegating work to qualified staff.

Action Tools

A vital part of a manager's job is to delegate assignments, along with decision-making authority, and to manage those assignments effectively. In carrying out this responsibility, a manager should keep in mind the following guidelines:

* Demonstrate trust in members of the team by delegating as much authority as they can handle.
* Develop employees and build their independence and initiative by entrusting them with both responsibility and authority.
* Relieve some of the pressure on his or her own time by delegating the day-to-day duties of the department to those who are willing and able to handle them.

5

Clarifying Delegated Assignments

Case Problem: "Don't Assume"

"Wait a minute! What the heck did Tom just say?" Jack, an industrial engineer, muttered to himself as he left his manager's office. "I know it's a vitally important assignment and that it's got to be done within three weeks, but what is it that I'm supposed to do?

"I can't believe my manager, Tom, just rushed through a complicated process in ten minutes without stopping to clarify any points. Then, without any discussion, it seems he expects me to understand the job as though I've been doing it for years. Well, that's impossible. It can't be done."

After an hour at his desk trying to make sense of the assignment, Jack, feeling frustrated, went into a colleague's office for help.

"Charlie, you've been an industrial engineer here now for over ten years," Jack began, "and you know the ins and outs of the operation. Help me. Our boss just gave me a vitally important assignment."

"So, what's the problem?" asked Charlie. "If it's that important, you should feel proud. Apparently, Tom trusts you well enough to think you can handle it."

"But that's just it, Charlie," replied Jack. "I've worked hard to earn Tom's trust; and now that I have it, I don't want to lose it.

"He rushed through a quick explanation of this assignment, mostly acknowledging his confidence in my ability. Then, he abruptly ended the meeting, ushered me out the door, and wished me well on this assignment. Not once did he stop to take a breath and ask me if I understood

14

the steps involved. He just assumed that I knew what he was talking about."

"Well, why didn't you stop him from talking and tell him you were confused?" asked Charlie. "If you needed clarification, you should have asked questions."

"I just couldn't do that at the time," responded Jack. "I would have made a fool of myself. That's why you've got to help me out. What should I do? Do you know anything about this job?"

Case Analysis

Jack's situation is certainly a rough one to be in. On the one hand, Jack has earned the trust of his manager. On the other hand, because of the communication breakdown between the two, Jack is bound to fail on this important assignment.

If Charlie, Jack's experienced co-worker, had worked on this job in the past, perhaps he would now come to Jack's rescue. But Charlie knows nothing about the job. Jack's options at this point are to suffer or to go back to his manager and admit his confusion.

Action Tools

To help delegate assignments as effectively as possible, consider the following action tools:

* Communicate assignments as clearly as possible. This means taking the time for questions and discussion to make certain your message is clearly understood.
* Do not assume. If you assume the listener is comprehending accurately and will carry out the action correctly, you will be wrong.
* Encourage all individuals who receive assignments from you to speak up, ask questions, and seek clarification until the assignments are absolutely clear.

6

Monitoring Employee Performance and Behavior

Case Problem: "Who's Watching the Shop?"

"I just don't know what's the matter with our colleague, Jan," said Ann to a fellow programmer analyst. "She used to be really interested in her work. It was always a pleasure to work with her. But something has definitely changed, and it's not for the better."

"You're absolutely right," responded Jeff. "In the past six months, Jan has completely changed. I just don't understand her one bit. If anything, she has succeeded in making me angry. Remember that management report that we were working on last week—the MIS project we worked day and night to complete? Well, if you recall, Jan was the only person who didn't stay and help out. In fact, she was the first one out the door to go off to her class or club meeting."

"I remember it well," Ann replied. "She doesn't even try to help out. I made the mistake of telling her that I got a raise. I thought she'd be happy for me, but was I wrong. She blew up and said she's the one around here who deserves a raise.

"For some reason, I felt guilty and told her I was sure she could get a raise if she would apply herself the way she used to. But she just glared at me and told me to mind my own business.

"I wish I understood the situation better. She and I go back a long time here. I don't like what I'm seeing, and I don't like the way things are headed."

Case Analysis

Things are not headed in the right direction for this team. Where is the manager of the MIS department? Who's watching the shop?

In this slice of life, we see the frustrations that occur when a respected colleague starts to change drastically for the worse.

Ann and Jeff care about the team that they once enjoyed and are now thrust into the dilemma of trying to figure out what is happening to their friend.

Jan is, in fact, changing. She once had been an achiever with realistic goals. Recently, however, Jan's perception of her job has changed. Many of her complaints and concerns have not been heard by her manager. As a result, she has become very bitter and disheartened.

Ann, Jeff, and Jan are the only long-term programmer analysts on the staff. In recent months, Jan has found herself dealing with many new employees and has received an increasing number of demands from upstairs that have intimidated her. Moreover, Jan has virtually disassociated herself from the others in her company by trying to find satisfaction through involvement in social activities and night school.

It is sad when such an obvious loss of a key player goes unnoticed by the manager. And equally as sad is that such oversights by management occur more often than imaginable.

Action Tools

Be aware of changes in employee work patterns, and be prepared to respond in the most helpful manner. To raise your awareness level and improve responsiveness to employee needs, consider the following action tools:

✳ Get to know each member of the staff individually. By regularly and openly communicating with employees, you will gain their trust and respect.

★ Together, set mutually agreed-upon goals. Remember, these goals must be achievable by the staff member— not by you.

★ Set up a regular follow-up system whereby you can monitor the progress of each individual's assignments.

★ Have the strength to give a "push" when necessary.

★ Have the wisdom and confidence to give appropriate rewards for a job well done.

7

Avoiding Misunderstanding in Delegation

Case Problem: "The Misunderstanding"

As he was rushing out of the office for his vacation, Terry, the director of financial planning, stopped Ralph, his senior financial analyst, in the hallway.

"Ralph," Terry said, "I'll be gone for a week and want you to personally take care of the Rhinehart thing for me." With that out of the way, Terry was off, confident that all business was being handled in his absence.Upon returning to the office, Terry asked Ralph to brief him on the Rhinehart matter.

"How did it turn out?" asked Terry.

"Oh, everything's fine now," responded Ralph.

"Good," said Terry, smiling. "So how is the new reporting system going?"

"The new what?" asked Ralph.

"The new financial reporting system project that Rhinehart is heading up," replied Terry. "You know that Jack, the senior vice president, has a great deal of respect for Rhinehart and believes Rhinehart will do a first-rate job heading up this project."

Not believing his ears, Ralph said, "Terry, this is the first I've heard of any of this. I had no idea I was supposed to get him reassigned to this project. There's been a terrible mistake."

"Terrible mistake?" asked Terry. "What did you do?"

"I did what I thought I was supposed to do—terminate Rhinehart!"

"You did what?" cried Terry. "How could you have done such a stupid thing? I never gave you such an order."

Trembling, Ralph tried to explain that two weeks ago, a rumor had circulated that Terry was dissatisfied with Rhinehart's work and was actively seeking a replacement for him. In addition, Ralph had overheard Terry telling the controller on the phone that Rhinehart was going to be pulled off all his current financial projects.

Upon hearing Ralph's explanation, Terry reacted saying, "Because you believed some stupid rumor and heard only part of my conversation, you assumed I was unhappy with Rhinehart and decided on your own to fire him. I can't believe what has happened."

Case Analysis

This case reveals that a serious business error has been made due to a series of communication breakdowns. Ralph fired Rhinehart without specific instructions from his boss to do so—a major error. However, despite Ralph's ineptitude and poor judgment, Terry cannot escape blame.

Let us examine how this error occurred:

- Terry gave incomplete orders and instructions to an employee while rushing out the door.
- Terry failed to give sufficient background information to Ralph.
- Terry failed to check out Ralph's understanding of the assignment.
- Ralph listened to rumors and believed them without checking out their accuracy.
- Ralph overheard only a brief part of a long, private conversation and drew erroneous conclusions.
- Ralph falsely assumed he had been given the supreme authority to fire an employee without clear and specific instructions to do so.

Action Tools

To help avoid misunderstanding when delegating, consider the following action tools:

* Take the proper amount of time to explain what is needed in a clear, unhurried manner.
* Always provide sufficient background and explanation to any employee concerning the reasons for an action.
* After giving instructions to an employee, always check out that individual's level of understanding.

8

Handling the End-Year Performance Reviews

Case Problem: "The Last Minute Reviews"

Last week, Alice started in her new position as customer service manager. She had left another company where she was a customer service team leader to take this promising job that offered real management responsibility and greater career opportunity. In so doing, she had promised herself to be the best manager possible.

Today, April 10, while having lunch with some of her customer service reps, she learns that their end-year reviews are always conducted in June. Carlos, one of her reps, asks, "Alice, a few of us were wondering how you will be able to do our reviews in June? It's only weeks away, and you're so new to the position and company."

Caught off guard by this question, Alice realizes that she and the center director never discussed in detail the subject of performance reviews. She explains that she will be discussing the subject of reviews at the Monday morning staff meeting.

As she walks back to her office, Alice wonders, "How am I going to put together these last-minute reviews and hold the performance review meetings in time? I don't know anything about these people."

Case Analysis

In this case, the new manager finds herself in a dilemma: either to do the reviews of people with whom she has no firsthand experience or to let the end-year reviews go, focusing instead on next-year's performance planning.

Over the past ten months, Alice's reps most likely have worked diligently, solved many business problems, developed themselves, and expended personal energy on behalf of the company. It is wrong, in this case, to cancel the end-year reviews simply because of a change in management. Such an action sends a message to employees that their efforts throughout the year are not important enough to be recognized.

The smarter solution for Alice is to move forward immediately in putting together the employee reviews, deal with the awkwardness of the situation as best as possible, and begin to build productive staff relationships now. This approach maintains the integrity and continuity of the performance management process and the credibility of management.

Action Tools

Many managers assume their positions toward the end of the year, with the challenge of end-year reviews just around the corner. If this happens to you, commit to the preparation and delivery of end-year reviews, and consider the following action tools:

- Ask your employees to provide you with their goals and information describing their performance throughout the year.
- Check with your manager for records of employee goal commitments and progress.
- Check with your predecessor, if possible, to obtain employee performance plans, including midstream reviews.
- Contact your human resources representative for employee performance information or prior reviews.
- Get performance feedback on employee contributions from leaders of teams on which your employees have served and from other recipients of their work.
- Check with peers of employees and gather their thoughts on each of your employees.

* If you manage supervisors, solicit feedback from their employees about the quality of each supervisor's effectiveness in directing work and developing people.
* Conduct participative performance reviews with employees. As part of this process, encourage each employee to describe his or her own accomplishments in meeting their goals. Then, share your findings about employee contributions and achievements, and negotiate to agreement those areas where there may be some difference of opinion.

Section II

Hiring and Other Staffing Responsibilities

9

The Staffing Side of Your Job

Case Problem: "The Rough Rider"

"I can't believe my ears!" exclaimed Alice, a candidate for the machine operator's position. "I've heard of men like you but didn't believe they existed. Where do you come off asking me personal questions like that?"

"Just cool your jets, Judy," replied Raymond, the production manager. "I was just making small talk and wanted. . . ."

"I'm not a Judy!" asserted Alice, cutting off Raymond abruptly. "My name is Mrs. Hernandez. And how dare you ask me where I was born, what church I belong to, and how many children I plan to have!"

"Look," said Raymond, "you people cause trouble wherever you go! Just get out of my office; there's no way you're gonna work for this company!"

After Alice had left, Raymond walked toward the snack area.

"Sure," he thought, "her resume looked fine, but what a nasty personality! I'm glad I found that out before hiring the broad."

Arriving at the snack area, Raymond was greeted by his boss, Chuck, the superintendent.

"Raymond," said Chuck, "I think we'd better talk about a problem that's come up. Let's go into my office."

Once in the office, Chuck explained the situation.

"This is an official complaint," Chuck said as he pointed to some papers on his desk. "According to Larry Jones, one of your operators, you treated him unfairly: You sent him home after only one verbal warning about his work."

"So what's wrong with that?" asked Raymond. "I'm his boss and I have that right."

"Yes, you are a production manager," said Chuck, "but Larry says that you usually give anyone else with the same problem three or four warnings, including written warnings, before taking such an action. In other words, Larry is claiming unfair treatment by you."

"That guy has some nerve to send this complaint to you, going over my head and behind my back," said Raymond angrily. "I told him my decision was final."

"That's another thing I wanted to mention to you," said Chuck. "When Larry gave me this complaint, he was extremely upset, claiming that you threatened him with serious repercussions should this matter go any farther. Did you?"

"Not really," responded Raymond, with embarrassment. "I may have been a little rough on the guy, but that was to set him straight as to who's production boss."

"Just as I thought," said Chuck. "We have a grievance procedure around here, and your job is to make sure that this procedure is used when problems can't be handled between you and your operators.

"You not only failed to inform Larry about this procedure, which is his right as an employee, but you also insinuated that reprisals would be taken if he made further efforts to resolve what he believed to be unfair treatment."

While Chuck was showing Raymond the written grievance procedure in the human resources policies manual, Randy and Josh, two other machine operators, were quietly commiserating behind closed doors.

"Two years ago," Randy confided in Josh, "I was sure I would be filling the senior operator's vacancy that had just opened up with the retirement of one of the old-timers. But to my surprise, Raymond went ahead on his own and hired some guy from the outside. I had the qualifications, had been with the company several years, and was mad as heck!"

"Well, I would be, too," responded Josh. "Isn't there a 'promote-from-within' policy here?"

"You bet," said Randy. "Right in the employee handbook. I took the matter to Chuck's office and contested the outside hiring. I even brought Simpson, the human resources director, into the dispute."

"What happened, did you win?" inquired Josh.

"I'm here, aren't I?" Randy stated proudly. "And I'm a senior operator. They fired that outsider just as fast as you can blink an eye and gave me the position, along with an apology from management."

After returning from a luncheon meeting, Raymond was relaxing at his desk when Paul Simpson, the human resources director, asked to come in and discuss an important matter.

"Raymond, we've got trouble," said Paul. "I don't like to be the bearer of bad news, but I just had a phone conversation with an attorney representing a Mrs. Alice Hernandez. He said she intends to file a lawsuit against you and the company because of unlawful and discriminatory practices against her by you in a job interview. Do you know what I'm talking about?"

"You and your dumb personnel rules, Simpson," retorted Raymond. "You're always on my back about this and that. The fact is that broad was crazy just like all those people!"

"I'm not here to defend myself, and I'm certainly not here to attack you at this time," asserted the human resources director. "Get this straight . . . we're in big trouble because of your actions with that job candidate and we had better sit down and start planning how to deal with this problem. And I'm telling you right now, Raymond, if we get through this one alive, you had better straighten up and start working with me, rather than against me."

Case Analysis

Raymond, a production manager, has a knack for getting in trouble while performing his staffing duties. He bungles interviewing, fair staff treatment, promoting and grievance procedures as well as his relationship with the human resources department.

During the selection interview with Alice Hernandez, Raymond wrongly attempted to engage in discussion of the candidate's personal background. Equal Employment Opportunity (EEO) guidelines clearly prohibit discussion of such matters as place of birth (national origin), religion, and family planning.

Raymond's ignorance—or perhaps rejection—of the EEO laws was strongly compounded by his overt bigotry toward females and/or Hispanics. In addition, his inept handling of the interview with Hernandez created serious legal complications.

The meeting between Raymond and his manager, Chuck, reveals Raymond's total disregard for the company's grievance procedure, which is clearly established in the company's human resources policies manual. Of great concern to Chuck was Raymond's refusal to let Larry, the subordinate, take his issue of unfair treatment any further as well as Raymond's threat of reprisals should Larry do this.

The entire philosophy of any grievance policy assumes that, on occasion, differences of opinion between employees and supervisors could arise that would require satisfactory resolution by other parties. Such a policy serves the best interests of employees as well as management by providing a clear means of problem-solving while protecting the chain of command concept.

The case of Josh, the new operator, presents additional indications of Raymond's inability to handle his staffing responsibilities. When hiring Josh, for example, Raymond failed to accurately describe the job Josh would be doing. The job description—had Raymond used one—would have been the perfect tool to help clarify Josh's job and prevent such a misunderstanding or misrepresentation.

In Randy's case, Raymond displayed a gross disregard for the published company policy of "promote from within" and rejected the human resources department as an important group to help in the recruitment and selection process. Had Raymond simply mentioned his need to fill the senior operator's vacant position to the human resources director, he would have been reminded of the "promote-from-within" policy.

A working relationship with human resources and an appreciation for its support services and professional staffing advice might have prevented not only the dispute over Raymond's wrongful hiring from outside but many of the staffing problems that he displayed in this case.

Action Tools

To effectively handle the staffing side of your job, consider the following action tools:

✦ Commit to excellence in staffing, recognizing that within your department, you may be accountable for everything from recruiting, selecting, hiring, orienting, placing, training, evaluating, promoting, disciplining, and compensating to the suspension or discharge of employees.

★ Obtain and maintain a current issue of the company's human resources policies manual as well as the employee handbook. Use your manual as a working guide to help ensure that daily staffing decisions made within your department are within human resources and legal guidelines.

★ Get to know the human resources professionals that support your department. These individuals possess special expertise to help you solve day-to-day people problems. They may also be able to provide you with specialized staffing services, such as recruiting and screening.

★ Be fair in handling performance problems with employees and implementing the company's system of progressive discipline, moving from oral to written warnings to suspension and discharge.

10

Retaining Final Authority in Hiring

Case Problem: "The Long-Distance Hire"

This is the fourth time over the past two months that Ed, the new drafter, failed to carry out his assigned duties. Mickey, the chief of mechanical engineering, has had it with Ed's ineptness, lack of professionalism and poor attitude toward the rest of the staff.

After disciplining Ed and warning him that such behavior would not be tolerated, Mickey called his senior drafter, Bob, into his office.

"Okay, Bob," Mickey said. "Where did you find that new guy? Two months ago, when I was on vacation, I trusted you to hire a competent drafter for me. And this is what you give me? I can't go on vacation for one week without something like this happening."

"Hold on just a minute," Bob replied defensively. "Two months ago, you left me holding the bag—instructing me to fill that vacancy— while you went to Tahiti for a week."

"Well, I should be able to trust you with something as important as a hiring decision," asserted Mickey. "You are my senior drafter, and you have been here longer than anyone else. You know the operations inside and out, and you should have done a better job in selecting a new person.

"Let's face facts. You didn't even ask anyone else in the department for an opinion about the three applicants you screened. You did a rush job and let me down!"

Case Analysis

Since Bob is the senior drafter and a trusted staffer, he could have been involved in the hiring process. However, it was wrong for the head of the group to fully delegate such a crucial management task to anyone else. The chief of mechanical engineering should have interviewed the candidate as well and made the final decision himself.

Action Tools

The selection and hiring of staff are responsibilities that must be handled by the manager—not delegated entirely to another individual in the department. In his or her team, the manager is ultimately accountable for the effectiveness of each member and should keep these points in mind:

- ✹ Retain the authority to make the final hiring decision.
- ✹ Be personally involved in the selection and hiring process.
- ✹ Get input from other members of the team regarding a candidate's credentials.
- ✹ Clearly explain the job specifications and required credentials to any staffer involved in the interviewing of job candidates.

11

Handling the Selection Interview

Case Problem: "Apply Here if You Dare"

After ten years as a field sales rep selling magazine advertising space for a mid-size publishing company, Larry Williams has been promoted to regional sales manager. One of his first responsibilities is to hire six sales reps to develop important new territories for the company.

This morning, Larry has his first job interview. The receptionist sends the candidate over to Larry's office at the appointed time. As the candidate enters Larry's office, Larry is on the phone and signals the man to come in and take a seat. With the candidate sitting in his office, Larry swings his chair away, facing the window. For fifteen minutes, he caustically reprimands a sales rep over the phone for not yet closing a new account, threatening the employee with a transfer to a smaller territory.

Hanging up the phone, Larry turns back to the man in his office, putting his feet up on his desk and his hands behind his head. He curtly introduces himself. "I'm Larry Williams, the regional sales manager, and you're Howard Corva. Is that right?"

The candidate nervously agrees.

"So, Mr. Corva," Larry continues, "what makes you so qualified to believe that you can handle a selling job with this company?"

"As you can see from my resume . . . ," the candidate responds. But Larry cuts him off gruffly.

"Mr. Corva, I don't have the time to study your resume and am asking you a direct question. Don't you know the answer without having to refer to your resume?"

The candidate is becoming very nervous and upset as Larry proceeds.

"Well, sir, let me ask you an easier question," says Larry. "You can travel, can't you?"

The candidate claims he can.

"Are you computer literate?" Larry asks. Howard Corva tries to answer by describing his computer knowledge and systems experience, but Larry cuts him off.

"Sir, understand something: I don't like talkative people," Larry says. "Just answer my question with a yes or no!"

"Yes!" responds the candidate, who is becoming increasingly irritated.

"I do remember seeing something on your application about your being involved in various community and professional associations," Larry reflects aloud, "Is that right?" The candidate nods affirmatively.

"Well, Mr. Corva, our sales people don't have time for such wasteful activities. Since you seem to have such outside interests, I just don't see how you'll have any time to do your work. Do you?"

Feeling highly defensive at this point, Howard Corva tries to answer the question. But at that moment, Larry's phone starts ringing. As Larry picks up the phone, he turns to the candidate and tells him he will have to go back to the reception area while he takes this call.

In response to Larry's direction, Howard Corva stands up to leave the office.

"Mr. Williams," Howard says, "I won't be waiting around any longer. You can take your bad attitude and give this lousy job to some loser who's willing to put up with your antics."

As the candidate leaves his office, Larry picks up the phone, realizing his national sales manager is on the other end.

"Hey, Larry, I forgot to mention something," says the sales manager. "You'll be interviewing a Howard Corva for a rep's position. I met him recently at a professional meeting. This guy's a real talent and can bring a lot of business to our company. I hope he joins us."

Case Analysis

In this case, a highly stressful job interview is conducted by a new manager who antagonizes and humiliates a talented candidate. As a result of Larry's sarcastic words, condescending attitude and rude behavior, Howard Corva becomes very upset and decides to cut his interview short.

Right from the beginning, everything seems to go wrong, convincing Howard that Larry is clearly the wrong manager to have and the company the wrong place to work. From Larry's fifteen-minute tirade to his superioristic body language to his harsh criticism and personal attack of Howard, we observe a job interview quickly disintegrating.

Action Tools

The selection interview is a critical opportunity for identifying qualified job candidates as well as a unique public relations opportunity for projecting an attractive picture of the job and company to prospective employees. To conduct an effective selection interview, consider the following action tools:

✦ Plan the selection interview by identifying key aspects or achievements of applicants about which you would like additional information and insights. Then, in the interviews, encourage applicants to discuss and develop these areas of interest. This can be done by using the following two-step approach:

  1. Begin with a general open-ended question, such as, "Tell me about your last job" or "Please discuss your experience in developing that new process."
  2. Then, follow up with a series of probing questions to elicit greater elaboration by the applicant. Such questions begin with words, such as what, where, when, why, who, and how.

✦ From the start, create a comfortable and cordial atmosphere that seeks to reduce anxiety and defensiveness rather than build unnecessary stress.
✦ Avoid directing or influencing an applicant's responses

by asking "leading" questions that suggest the desired answers. Instead, keep questions objective. Allow the applicant to respond freely without feeling obligated to follow any suggested lead. For example, don't ask, "You do like XYZ computers, don't you?" Instead, ask, "What brand of computer do you like?"

★ Avoid squelching an applicant's free expression of thoughts by making him or her feel defensive, guilty, or angry because of critical or judgmental statements, such as, "You are absolutely wrong and should be embarrassed to say such a thing," or "I can't imagine where you got such ridiculous ideas," or "You don't know what you're talking about!"

★ Ask "open-ended" questions that require detailed responses. Avoid "close-ended" questions that result in yes/no answers and thereby discourage further responses.

★ Encourage job applicants to do most of the talking during job interviews. Remember, the main objective of the interview is to gather sufficient knowledge of job candidates to allow you to make intelligent hiring decisions.

★ Always act with courtesy and respect. The selection interview should send a clear message to all candidates that your company is a positive, friendly, and professional place to work.

12

Considering the Nontechnical Social Factors in Hiring

Case Problem: "The Shining Star"

Upset about the unexpected meeting that had just occurred in his office, Tom, director of new product development, walked over to the office of Eric, a senior research engineer in the department.

"You won't believe what just happened," he said. "Sam, the newest member of our department, just up and quit."

"Well," replied Eric, "I've got to be honest. Bets were out he wouldn't have lasted this long."

"What are you talking about?" asked Tom.

"Admit it, Tom," said Eric, "the guy was discontented from the very beginning. I didn't get the impression he was ready to work with characters like Ernie and Max. And besides, you knew he was single, and this is a very settled area with almost no social activities for single people."

"Look, Eric, we need good people here," Tom said defensively. "Sam was very competent and eager to come on board."

"I don't like to say I told you so," said Eric, "but remember we'd agreed to get department input on hiring to 'feel out' the different candidates because we've had the same type of problems in the past."

"Maybe I should have gotten some input," admitted Tom. "I was just so enthusiastic about Sam's technical background that I didn't want to wait."

"By the way, what were his reasons for leaving?" asked Eric.

"Well," replied Tom, "he said that while he liked the work and the people he worked with, he felt frustrated because his family and friends lived so far away. And as a single person in this town, he had no opportunity to meet other singles."

"Did he say anything about the rural location of our plant?" asked Eric. "You know, Tom, the fellow lived in Philadelphia all his life, and I had wondered if that transition would be hard to make."

"Yes," replied Tom, "he did mention that hardship but felt that a good social situation might have compensated for it. There was just nothing I could say, Eric. He had his mind made up. I guess I was just too shortsighted and too quick in making up my mind."

Case Analysis

Sam's grievances should not have surfaced in the form of a resignation. This situation might have been prevented in the hiring process. As the senior research engineer pointed out to his boss, participation by other staff members in the selection process might have revealed the new employee's concerns about his social life. In addition, the director of new product development should have openly shared as much information as possible about the company, its community and lifestyle.

In a hiring situation, it is tempting to focus attention on—and overly emphasize—technical credentials, while paying too little attention to the candidate's personal and social concerns.

Action Tools

Consider the following action tools in the hiring process:

 As a buyer of talent for the department, the manager must screen each candidate on a number of important factors. In addition to exhibiting the necessary technical capabilities, a job candidate must possess interests and preferences in line with the company's geographic location, community lifestyle, and other social-related matters.

✴ During the interviewing process, the manager should control any impulse to make quick judgments on "shining star" candidates—seemingly outstanding applicants—and be certain to fully discuss and assess all aspects of each individual.

✴ The manager can gain valuable information by assembling a staff selection team to assist in the selection effort. Such a team can provide invaluable information and contribute many different helpful insights to create a total profile of the candidate.

13

Orienting New and Transferred Employees

Case Problem: "The Disoriented Employee"

"John, can I sit here and talk with you a few minutes while you're having lunch?" asked Mary of a fellow accountant who had joined the firm only three months earlier.

"Why? Did I do something wrong?" responded John, defensively.

"No," said Mary. "Well, I mean, the other folks in the department and I were wondering why you haven't tried to join in the group or get to know us better—we're really a nice bunch to work with, you know."

"It's nothing personal, Mary," explained John. "It's just that I feel like the new guy on the block and all of you always seem so busy. I guess I also thought you folks didn't really take to new people that easily. You're the first person I've had any kind of social talk with since I arrived."

"Well, I'm really glad we're talking now," smiled Mary. "The fact is you just seemed to appear on the job one day—the boss didn't introduce you to us or tell us anything about you. And then we never seemed to see you around.

"Look, John, the rest of the accounting staff is sitting over there. Why don't you come over and join us. I think this is a good time for all of us to get to know you."

With that, John walked over with Mary and joined the group for lunch and conversation. Within a few minutes, everyone at the table realized that John's feelings of isolation were unnecessary and could have been avoided had the accounting manager merely informed the staff of John's employment before he arrived and made some effort to introduce and involve John as a new, important addition to accounting.

"You know, something similar happened to me when I joined the staff four years ago," recalled Mike, another accountant. "It took me about half a year to really get acquainted with the physical facilities and some of the key people I would be interfacing with in other areas. In fact, now that I look back, had the manager or even human resources just given me a guided tour of the facility—and introduced me to the staff, I'm sure I would have adjusted faster and accomplished a lot more since coming on board."

"I understand exactly what you folks are saying," interjected Rob, a six-year senior accountant. "My first year here was difficult for me. I was transferred from another division on the West Coast with no knowledge about this company, its products, procedures or this job.

"Because I had been in accounting for a few years prior to coming here and had worked within the same parent company, the accounting manager assumed I didn't need any help in getting started. Well, was he wrong! He never gave me a job description or any written operating procedures, even though I asked. He said, 'You know what to do. You've worked in accounting long enough. And, furthermore, those things will only restrict you.' "Six months later, during my first performance review, I was destroyed for not fully understanding my job duties and operating procedures and for putting emphasis on the wrong assignments."

Case Analysis

As the staff shared similar stories of early frustration and failure on the job, it became clear that, in all cases, their problems could have been prevented had their manager personally taken the lead in providing each new staffer with a carefully planned orientation.

While human resources specialists are often assigned to provide basic orientation to the company and its employee policies, only the department manager can make sure that each person joining the staff is completely familiar and comfortable with the job, the work group, and the organization as well as the community.

Action Tools

The orientation process is of vital importance and can help ensure successful integration of new talent and personalities into an existing departmental structure. A manager's failure to personally coordinate each new staffer's orientation in a comprehensive and wholehearted manner is certain to lead to early staff frustration and possible job failure. With this in mind, the manager should:

* Help each employee become familiar with the job, the work group, the organization, and the community.
* Plan an orientation to begin before the staff member actually comes on board. If a geographic relocation is involved, the manager should help familiarize the individual with the community and its resources.
* Plan an orientation that will continue up to six months after employment, with regular follow-up to ensure proper and healthy adjustment to the new situation.
* Introduce the new staffer to coworkers and other important individuals in the organization. In addition, encourage others to help break in the new staffer and make him or her feel a part of the company team.
* Provide all job and procedural guidelines, such as job descriptions, operating manuals, employee handbooks, and organization charts, to help the new employee gain a clear understanding of the job and the organization's dynamics.
* Make certain the new employee has filled out all necessary forms and clearly understands all human resources policies and practices.
* Never assume that the human resources department is handling the orientation for you. Proper orientation is the manager's responsibility. While human resources can provide initial assistance with the company-wide orientation, the manager must be responsible for fully planning and implementing the departmental orientation.

14

Providing Guidance and Support to New Employees

Case Problem: "New Kid on the Block"

"I've tried again and again to make things work, but with no success. That's why I've come to see you," bemoaned Gary, a sales associate of three months, to Max, the assistant store manager. "I've tried to talk with Bob, my manager, but he breaks appointments and is virtually impossible to get hold of."

"Look Gary," Max interrupted, "sit down, cool off, and tell me what the problem is. You've been here just a few months, and it can't be all that bad, can it?"

Seeing that Max was willing to listen, Gary sat down and related the events leading up to this blow-up. Since coming on board as a new salesperson, Gary had found himself abandoned by his manager and floundering alone.

His coworkers, a tightly knit group, had worked together for eight years, with their loyalty primarily directed toward Al, a senior salesperson in the department. Unfortunately for Gary, Al took an immediate dislike to him, resulting in Gary's alienation from the rest of the group.

On various occasions, Gary sought advice from his coworkers and even attempted to join them for lunch, only to be ignored or belittled. On a number of occasions, he sought help from Bob, but Bob also put him off. There seemed to be no help anywhere. Alone, alienated, and filled with anger, Gary finished telling his story to Max.

"Look Gary," Max empathized, "this is a terrible way to feel, especially working for this department store where we take pride in teamwork and value our employees. Do me a favor and hold tight. I'll check this out and will get back in touch with you by tomorrow afternoon."

As soon as Gary had left, Max called Bob into his office and related Gary's story to him. Somewhat defensively, Bob explained that he knew nothing of Gary's trouble and frustrations and just assumed that Gary, although the youngest and newest member of the department, could fend for himself.

Amazed at his manager's lack of awareness of Gary's situation, Max directed Bob to talk to Gary and resolve the problem. Max pointed out that the maintenance of healthy human relations and effective teamwork were department management responsibilities. He concluded the discussion by reminding Bob that when he started working for the company fifteen years ago, "I made you feel at home and gave you all the help and understanding you needed—you didn't have to fend for yourself then."

Case Analysis

A new employee should not be allowed to flounder helplessly, especially when capable managers and colleagues are available to provide guidance and support. As department manager, Bob failed to respond to the pleas of a new sales associate, allowing existing group dynamics to pose a major obstacle to Gary's performance and well-being.

Fortunately for Gary though, Max, the assistant store manager, exhibited sensitivity and leadership in responding to the problem at hand. While listening to Gary's story and reassuring him that the problem would be addressed, Max refrained from personally attempting to resolve Gary's problem. Such a personal action by Max would have undermined the department head's responsibility in the clothing department. Max correctly informed Bob of the situation and requested that Bob take immediate corrective action to resolve Gary's problem.

Action Tools

It is the manager's responsibility to assure successful integration of new employees into the department team. This can be achieved by implementing the following tips:

* Solicit the cooperation of all department members in providing assistance to any new member of the team.
* Request special assistance from informal group leaders in orienting new employees and making them feel welcome.
* Keep your antenna up to monitor the personal chemistry and relationships within the group.
* Commit to support and guide new employees, especially during their early months on the job.
* Be responsive to calls for help from employees and particularly accessible to new employees in their times of need.

15

Setting High Departmental Standards as a New Manager

Case Problem: "The Bitter Beginning"

While having lunch in the company cafeteria, Jack, the general credit manager and a twelve-year veteran, couldn't wait to tell his friend, Marv, a sales representative, about the new controller's first divisional management meeting.

"You wouldn't believe what the new guy said," Jack said angrily. "Let me see if I can recall some of his 'pearls of wisdom.'

"The new boss said, 'Okay, you guys, now that I'm in charge, let's get one thing clear. I've checked you out, and just by looking at you, I can tell my sources weren't too far off. So you won't be pulling the wool over my eyes like you did with my predecessor—who, by the way, is a good friend of mine. I want to tell you about yourselves.

" 'Your past record is a disgrace, demonstrating indifference to the company's needs, as well as a lack of interest in our division. In fact, it seems to me that all you've been demonstrating around here has been laziness, avoidance of work and, in some cases, just plain stupidity.' "

"Jack, you've got to be kidding," Marv interrupted. "You're putting me on!"

"No, I'm not, Marv," Jack replied. "But wait, it gets better. The new controller also said, 'I've been brought in to whip this group into shape. This is how I'm going to do it.

" 'First, although I don't expect good performance from any of you, I'd better get it, or else. Second, if you don't perform satisfactorily,

47

you're going to be in for some big trouble. And, third, if, by some stroke of luck, you manage to succeed in improving this division's performance, don't look to me for any "thank you's"—you'll only be doing what you're getting paid for.' "

"Well, Jack," said Marv, "it seems as though hard times are ahead for you and the rest of your division. Tolerate this guy as long as you have to; but if I were you, I'd start looking around for a new opportunity. I just don't see how you can come out winning."

Case Analysis

It is difficult to imagine any employee winning with a manager like the new controller. Even if Jack and his colleagues try to improve the division's performance, they probably won't make much headway with their new boss, since he already is convinced that they are losers and has no confidence in their ability to turn the division around.

In addition, he has refused to offer his management staff any incentive for working harder, informing them that they will receive no recognition for improved performance.

Action Tools

The initial expectations and attitudes communicated by a new manager to a department can be extremely important in setting the direction for the staff. To help start off your new relationship with employees in a positive and productive manner, consider the following action tools:

- During your initial staff meeting, create a positive mood and share your vision for teamwork and top results.
- Explain your goals for the department and share preliminary guidelines for successful operations.
- Explain your high standards and expectations of top performance and dedication to quality.
- Inform your staff that top efforts and significant contributions to the department will be recognized.
- Let your staff know that you are there to support and encourage them.

16

Utilizing Temporary and Part-Time Workers

Case Problem: "The Second-Class Citizen"

Five years ago, Lola, a successful marketing manager, resigned her position to raise her new baby daughter. After four-and-a-half years of caring for her child full time, Lola decided to return to work doing temporary marketing assignments for a national temp firm. For the past six months, she has worked at three different companies and found the work exciting and challenging.

Two months ago, Lola's husband, Elwood, an experienced accountant with a major corporation, lost his job in a corporate downsizing. As a result of his job loss, Lola and Elwood decided it would be best if Elwood could also take on temp assignments for the next few years. This way, both could spend time with their daughter and share family responsibilities.

And so, Elwood signed on with a local temporary agency, specializing in accounting and bookkeeping. Unfortunately, after just four weeks on his first assignment, Elwood reveals to Lola: "That's it! I've had it as a temp and as a second-class citizen! I'm getting out of the temporary business and going back to a full-time accounting position."

"Elwood, what's going on that would get you this upset and make you want to give up on our plans in such a short time?" Lola inquires.

"Here, Lola, read for yourself," replies Elwood, pulling a notebook out of his briefcase. "I've created a daily work journal and have circled in red various entries that will explain my feelings."

Sept. 18: It's been a week since I've started working here; and Linda, the assistant controller, still hasn't formally introduced me to any of the managers or staff in the department. They don't even know my name and call me Elbert . . . Elvis . . . Eggbert . . . What's your name or Hey you!

Sept. 20: I keep getting dumped on by everyone. The piles on my desk are getting too high. I try to tell them I'm supposed to be working on the "management and consolidation reporting project," but they don't listen and don't seem to care.

Sept. 24: It's been two weeks, and I'm still wearing my visitor's badge. When will I get the proper security clearance? I can't go anywhere alone without proper clearance—not to the cafeteria . . . not even to the rest room. Linda says getting clearance takes a while. But how long? And every time I ask to be escorted somewhere, people get irritated with me, telling me that I'm inconveniencing them.

Sept. 27: The staff just celebrated an employee's birthday in the large conference room, and I wasn't invited. The only one in the department . . . what a downer!

Sept. 28: I've received very little feedback on my work from Linda since starting. I leave her e-mails, voice messages, and memos. She's just never around and doesn't respond to my calls.

Oct. 2: I haven't attended any of the staff meetings. I've been informed that they're only for full-time employees. But I know I'm missing a lot of important information that might help me out on my project.

Oct. 5: I eat lunch alone each day in the company cafeteria. The accounting staff has never asked me to join them.

Oct. 8: I met three other temporary workers at lunch today. I couldn't believe it . . . they had similar war stories. And they work in other departments and for other agencies.

Oct. 12: Today, I noticed a problem with the com-

pany's order fulfillment process that the system improvement team is working on. When I informed one of
the accountants on that team of my discovery, he told
me that I was just a temp and they knew what they
were doing.

Lola stopped reading and looked up.

"Elwood, I am so sorry," she said, "I didn't know. Why didn't you
tell me about these things?"

"You have your responsibilities, and I figured things would improve," Elwood responded.

"Why didn't you contact the temp firm you're working for?" Lola
asked.

Elwood explained that he had, but that the assignment manager
was abrupt and told him to "do whatever the client wants." And when
he called a second time to ask for help, the same person threatened
him by saying, "Look, if you can't do what our client wants, we might
have to reconsider you for future assignments!"

"Elwood, enough is enough!" said Lola, angrily. "You don't need
that assignment any longer. And you certainly don't need to be treated
like some second-class citizen by that miserable agency. Let's work together to find you the right firm with the right attitude. Maybe my firm
would be a good place to start looking."

Case Analysis

A huge and growing force in American business is the supplementary workforce. It is composed of millions of highly skilled
and flexible individuals classified as independent contractors,
part-time and temporary employees, temporary agency workers,
consultants, and freelancers. These supplementary professionals
provide a strategic and competitive advantage to corporations
who must respond rapidly to the shifting demands of a fast-
paced global marketplace. Today's successful staffing formula
combines a solid, loyal, professional core of full-time employees
with a highly flexible and skilled supplementary workforce.

In Elwood's case, it is clear that his current assignment is
with a company whose managers do not understand the strategic value of flexible staffing. In addition, the managers appear

to be totally inept at managing supplementary workers and creating a harmonious and productive environment in which both full-time professionals and supplementary workers can work effectively together.

In this poorly managed situation, everyone loses. The accounting department loses a skilled and caring worker. The assistant controller loses by not having a critical project completed on time. And, of course, Elwood loses.

Action Tools

To effectively manage supplementary workers, consider the following action tools:

- ✦ Provide supplementary workers with an orientation to the business. Make them feel a part of the company by giving them a brief tour of the facilities and introducing them to various managers and employees. Also, explain your company's mission, history, markets, products, services, and practices.
- ✦ Make your temporary workers feel a part of your department by introducing them to your full-time staff and by briefing your staff on the nature of their temporary assignments. Then, give your new workers a brief department tour, reviewing departmental projects, key contacts in other areas, and key numbers, including phone, fax, and e-mail. Also review the equipment and other resources available to them.
- ✦ Assign your supplementary workers to full-time employees who will be accountable for delegating work to them, seeing that their assignments are completed properly, and introducing them to the work group. Remember to recognize those staff members who help with this important contribution.
- ✦ Give sincere and immediate praise when you observe supplementary workers extending themselves. When superior levels of achievement are exhibited, put your praise in writing, giving commendations to the workers

involved as well as to the managers of their firms, if they are employed by temporary staffing or consulting firms.

✱ Include temporary workers in department and team meetings. They are part of your group and need project updates, scheduling information, and other business information relevant to the group's work.

✱ Protect temporary workers from being "dumped on" by anyone in the department. Unless you clarify to your full-time staff the assignments of your temporary workers, these new people may feel obliged to accept dumped work and will quickly become overwhelmed.

✱ If you plan to staff short-term, peak season or special project needs through temporary staffing firms, check with managers in your company and in other companies in your community to gather names of reputable firms and business references.

✱ When calling a firm, initially screen for courtesy and professionalism. Find out the firm's length of time in business and ask for references and customer surveys. Also, ask about the firm's recruiting, testing, training, compensation and benefits arrangements for their temporary employees. Firms often offer attractive and comprehensive training and benefits programs to help attract and retain the best temporary workers.

✱ Meet with the manager of the firm and carefully review your specific staffing requirements. Make certain their people possess the skills you seek and would be available on the dates you request. In addition, invite the firm's manager to your facility to acquaint this individual with your organization's needs, processes, standards, and culture.

Section III

Team-Building Responsibilities

17

Building High-
Performance Teamwork

Case Problem: "Changing Paradigm"

Six months ago, Mark, a senior systems analyst with eight years of experience, assumed a position as manager with the Information Management Department. Today, he received his first management performance review from his director, Ken.

Back at his desk, Mark reread the written performance summary. His group met most of their technical objectives for the period—but just marginally. In particular, Mark was very disappointed about his low rating on "Building High Performance Teamwork."

In the meeting, Ken reminded Mark of how important teamwork was to the company. Just last year, the president had announced his new vision for the business: "A customer-driven high performance team organization staffed by high-involvement teams and winning partnerships."

There was no denying the facts; the observations, comments and examples of poor teamwork said it all. Mark had to start turning things around in the next six months. Fortunately, Ken was willing to work closely with him in putting together a performance improvement plan.

The agreement was for Mark to review the report and come up with solid recommendations for improving teamwork. Ken would also try to come up with some ideas. Then, in a week, both would get together and agree upon a performance improvement plan for Mark's group.

Mark sat there thoughtfully as he reviewed Ken's negative assessment of his group's teamwork:

- There is little or no shared understanding of goals, problems, or processes.
- Very little concern is shown for the views or feelings of others.
- Members tend to confine themselves to their own jobs.
- People do not support each other with the necessary information, resources, or assistance.
- Leadership of the group is dominated by the manager.
- The group has very low morale and cohesiveness.
- There is no sense of team identity or pride.
- No team development activities are provided.

Case Analysis

The best companies in the world have discovered the teamwork advantage and are rapidly changing their approach to work and management. Preoccupation with hierarchy and bureaucracy are giving way to a focus on customers and teamwork.

To meet the requirements of the new customer-driven team environment, managers must become effective team builders and team leaders, able to transform groups of individuals into focused and dynamic high performance teams.

Mark has been reminded by his director, Ken, of the importance of teamwork. The examples of poor teamwork given to him during his first management performance review are clearly unacceptable behaviors that limit the potential of his work group to perform at optimum levels.

Fortunately, Ken is a supportive and intelligent team leader and coach who is willing to work with Mark as a partner to help turn things around. If Mark puts together a solid performance improvement plan for enhancing teamwork and enthusiastically carries it out, the prognosis for improving team dynamics and results in his work group is excellent.

Action Tools

To develop a high performance team environment, consider the following action tools:

✴ Recruit and hire individuals with "high tech" skills and "high touch" ability. Remember, technical expertise without the ability to successfully team and partner with others may quickly become a liability to your department.

✴ Provide formal team training to your entire group—including yourself—on how to create a high performance team and how to operate as an effective team leader and member on a day-to-day basis.

✴ Provide clear expectations and priorities for teamwork, and hold each employee personally accountable for demonstrating team behavior during daily work activities. If employees perform well, recognize them. If they fail to meet expectations, provide immediate and honest coaching.

✴ Give employees a sense of departmental ownership by sharing your group's goals, such as production, quality, costs, safety, schedule, and improvements. Have employees work with you in tracking departmental progress.

✴ Get employees involved in problem-solving activities. When the team's progress is being hindered, form cross-department improvement teams to address those situations. When individuals are experiencing difficulties in their jobs, use a portion of team meetings to have team members offer help to fellow employees in need.

✴ Encourage employees to share leadership of the group. This can be done by asking for help in the running of regular team meetings and also by soliciting team leaders to coordinate department-wide improvement projects.

✴ Keep employees fully informed about all aspects of the department, including plans, processes, results, and problems; customer requirements and feedback; relations with other departments; new management strategies and approaches; and the state of the business as a whole.

✴ Encourage your employees to develop a team "Code of Conduct" for acting properly as a team in meetings.

Such a code of Dos and Don'ts—if created and enforced by the employees themselves—is a great tool for maintaining professional team behavior.

★ Help your employees understand and support the whole team system by instituting appropriate cross-training and providing multi-skilling opportunities.

18

Coordinating the Department's Staff and Work

Case Problem: "The Uncoordinated Manager"

"No sir," said Phil, the purchasing manager, at the management team meeting, "this time I won't sit by quietly and take the blame for shutting down production because of a lack of supplies. It's accounting's fault, and Sam knows it."

"Don't point fingers," responded Sam, the plant controller, angrily. "We do our best."

"Just pay those bills on time when you're supposed to," returned Phil. "Then, perhaps, I won't have so many hold-ups in the delivery of needed materials for production by our vendors. You guys in accounting are messing up my relationship with our key suppliers."

"That's enough now," interrupted John, the general manager. "Just stop it! We'll take this problem of coordination up privately later—just the three of us. But we'd better learn to start cooperating. I don't like these outbursts and attacks among my staff. We're supposed to be a management team. So let's act like professionals and get on with business."

After the meeting broke up, the general manager checked out a hunch. He met privately with his engineering manager and then with his industrial relations director.

"I don't like to complain about anyone, but the fact is that Sam, on occasion, fails to pay our suppliers on time," the engineering manager explained. "When I've tried to resolve the problem directly, Sam becomes defensive and argues with me."

"Sam was supposed to be collaborating with me in the negotiation of insurance contracts under our employee benefits program," confided the industrial relations director. "But every time I needed to get together with him, he was too busy. I just don't feel as though he really cares to work with me on this project. You know that I need his financial expertise."

Following his private meetings, John, the general manager, checked Sam's employee fact file, trying to recall Sam's major problems of the past year and improvement plans for the current year.

"Now I see what's happening," thought John.

Getting on the phone, John called Sam into the office. A minute later, Sam arrived, upset from the earlier dispute and somewhat anxious about the meeting.

"Sam, sit down and relax," invited John. "I'm not here to attack you, but to discuss your progress on a commitment you made to me six months ago in last year's performance review. Do you remember?"

"Well, yes, I think I do," recalled Sam. "My problems had to do with internal accounting matters."

"To be exact, Sam," clarified John, "your problems dealt with lack of coordination within the accounting department. As you may recall, in my questioning of the accounting staff, your people didn't seem to understand the major goals of the department last year. Also your department lacked any sort of written job descriptions or coordinating guidelines."

"But those problems have been corrected," Sam responded quickly. "All accounting plans are known by everyone. In addition, each person has a clear job description, and I'm currently working up a set of internal accounting procedures."

"OK, that's good," smiled John. "I also note that last year you had a problem with assigning staff to projects. One project was composed of three people who were mismatched, not only technically but also interpersonally. Have you done anything about that?"

"I have," answered Sam. "I know that the assignment of staff to projects and jobs is an important responsibility, and I'm on top of it. . . . I assure you!"

"Good," replied John. "And have your scheduling and back-up problems been taken care of, too? Do you remember the time that everyone in the department was either on vacation, at the accounting conference or at training sessions? You were the only person left to do the department's work."

"Yes," replied Sam. "All assignments are now better planned, and my staff is better scheduled. In fact, each of my senior people, including myself, has a back-up in place to handle contingencies."

"Sounds good, Sam," John nodded, looking pleased. "It seems as though you are coordinating your department, people, and work a lot better than last year. But I must point out that you have two responsibilities for coordination—the internal coordination of your department and the coordination of accounting with all other departments.

"While your internal coordination problem is being handled, which I appreciate, I think we'd better talk about your interdepartmental responsibility to deal effectively with other areas of the company in a coordinated fashion. After all, we're all part of the management team. Do you understand?"

"You bet, John. I'm ready to improve myself there, too!"

Case Analysis

As John, the general manager, correctly points out, the accounting manager has two coordination responsibilities:

1. Internal coordination within the accounting department.
2. Interdepartmental coordination of accounting with all other areas of the company in pursuit of company objectives.

After the flare-up between the purchasing manager and the controller at the management team meeting, John's hunch about Sam's continuing coordination problems was confirmed. This was done through discussions with the engineering manager and industrial relations director and an examination of the employee fact file. Since last year's major problem dealt with the need for better internal coordination, it seemed plausible that Sam's current problems stemmed from the same root cause—lack of coordination skills.

John's meeting and discussion with Sam is an excellent example of concerned, threat-free counseling that should effectively win Sam's cooperation in committing to develop better interdepartmental procedures and management cooperation.

Action Tools

The manager has the responsibility for coordinating the internal efforts and activities of the staff and the external relationships of the department as it works with other key areas of the company to contribute to overall corporate objectives. In this regard, the manager should:

- ✴ Fully discuss departmental plans with the staff who will carry them out, allowing individuals to voice their opinions and contribute suggestions to the plans. This provides opportunities for clear understanding of and commitment to goals by members of the staff.
- ✴ Coordinate the organization of staff work. This refers to "who does what with whom, when, where and how." Organizational coordination involves development of clear job descriptions and operating procedures.
- ✴ Handle the staffing function in a coordinated manner so that the department has the right number of people to perform the needed jobs with the necessary competencies.
- ✴ Direct the staff by providing essential coordinating instructions on a regular basis so that all employees work together harmoniously in reaching departmental goals in the most efficient manner.
- ✴ Regularly observe and discuss employee performance with staff members. Determine when actual results deviate from planned performance and take immediate corrective action. Such action may involve on-site coaching or formal training.
- ✴ Work cooperatively with fellow managers of your management team to continuously improve interdepartmental coordination, work flow, and relationships.

19

Moving to Self-Directed Work Teams

Case Problem: "Poof . . . You're a Team Leader"

Three months ago, Jim, a manufacturing plant manager, along with members of senior management, attended a university course on world-class manufacturing strategies. Upon returning home, Jim called a staff meeting of all managers and supervisors in the plant.

He was excited about the many new approaches and ideas for improving productivity and controlling costs in the workplace. In particular, he felt that the concept of self-directed work teams could easily fit into the plant's work environment and support the company's goals.

One week later, Jim sent out the following memo to the plant supervisors:

To All Plant Supervisors:

As mentioned in my staff meeting last week, I believe that the self-directed team approach holds out great promise for improving our productivity, controlling costs, and eliminating unnecessary positions at the work-group level.

Therefore, as of this coming Monday, your work groups will be referred to as self-directed work teams, and all supervisors will be known as team leaders.

As team leaders, you will no longer provide day-to-day supervision of employees and direction of work. Instead, our employees will handle these responsibilities themselves.

**In six months, we will review our progress. At that time, I
expect each work team to be completely self-directed and all
formal team leader positions to be eliminated as a result. Those
team leaders who have succeeded in helping their teams become
self-managed may be considered for other positions in the plant
or in other company facilities.**

Thank you for your assistance.

Three months later, three team leaders shared their feelings about
the move to self-directed teams.

"I've completely stopped giving directions to my workers, as we
were ordered to do," began Joel. "But at what price? Our productivity
is way off, there are lots of arguments among the employees, and my
two best workers are talking about quitting."

"I've really tried hard to be nondirective and encourage the workers to take on more responsibility," Yolanda joins in. "But it's just not
happening. My employees are nice, quiet people who have depended
upon me for years. I feel so guilty about not helping them out. I just
hate this job since Jim started all this team stuff."

"I'm completely frustrated by not being able to do my job and su-
pervise my work group as I've always done," agrees Paul. "One day, I'm
a successful supervisor. The next day, I get a memo from the boss saying, 'Poof, you're a team leader!' And, if I'm successful in helping create
teamwork here, what's in it for me? I'll probably get canned!"

Case Analysis

More and more companies are teaming up their workforces and
seeking total employee involvement in a search for better quality, improved productivity, greater customer satisfaction, and
enhanced overall profitability. From a leadership perspective,
companies can design their front-line work teams to be "manager-led" or "self-directed" by the employees themselves.

In the manager-led work team model, day-to-day leadership of the group continues to be handled by the group's direct
manager. However, the manager works with employees in implementing a systematic team-building process to maximize employee involvement and empowerment and to help employees
feel greater ownership over many aspects of the team's processes.

In the self-directed work team (SDWT) model, employees assume most or all of the day-to-day leadership duties of the team. In self-directed work team facilities, there are fewer managers but more individuals who play important team support roles, including facilitating, counseling, coaching, resourcing, training, and removing cross-functional barriers.

In the case above, three manufacturing supervisors were ordered to stop utilizing their customary and traditional supervisory skills to help change their organization to one of self-directed work teams. The supervisors were unclear and confused about their new roles, frustrated by their inability to help employees get the work out and solve group problems, and depressed about the future uncertainty of their jobs with the company.

Unfortunately, this rapid changeover to teams will probably fail due to poor communications, unrealistic time lines, a nonexistent team-building implementation process, total lack of training, and nonsupportive management, along with prospects of job losses should the changeover succeed. Unless Paul, Yolanda, and Joel can talk seriously with the plant manager and convince him to review and improve the change process for building work teams, further deterioration of current operations and failure to achieve self-directed work teams will occur.

Action Tools

If your organization is contemplating a move toward self-directed work teams, consider the following action tools:

- ✴ Senior management should articulate a clear vision about where it wants the organization to go—an empowered self-directed work team organization—and how it intends to get there.
- ✴ All managers and employees should be given a clear and measurable step-by-step team-building implementation plan with guideposts and milestones to mark the way.
- ✴ Each team manager or supervisor should develop a

gradual hand-off plan listing current team manager responsibilities and future team leadership responsibilities that will be progressively assumed by team members.

✴ All individuals involved in the changeover to self-directed work teams should participate in formal team training courses that show the strategic change process and provide specific team-building skills and activities for implementing the change.

✴ Employees should attend specialized workshops dealing with specific team processes and skills, such as meeting leadership and dynamics, problem-solving and decision-making, communication, assertiveness, and conflict management.

✴ Employees should become skilled in a number of the team's technical roles. Cross-training will provide each employee with broader skill sets that will foster greater flexibility in helping teams meet changing demands.

✴ As self-directed work teams are phased in and front-line managerial or supervisory positions are phased out, the organization should ensure that those who helped in the changeover are provided with opportunities for promotion, changes into support roles, relocation to other facilities, transition back to technical jobs, or possibly even attractive early retirement programs.

✴ Management should provide reasonable and realistic timelines for progressing through the planned phases toward self-direction. Depending upon the degree of bureaucracy and hierarchy, as well as the size of the organization involved, the timeline for creating a high performance self-directed work team environment could run anywhere from one-and-a-half to three years.

20

Managing Change

Case Problem: "A Lack of Buy-In"

At the monthly meeting of a local management association, managers from different companies are describing current changes being implemented within their organizations and the reactions of their people to these changes. Here's what Diane, a customer service manager, has to say:

"Our organization is undertaking a reengineering of its business processes to improve our key measures, including quality, costs, speed, and customer satisfaction.

"Customer service work was formerly carried out by a variety of people working in different departments for different bosses. Now, the same work is handled as a single integrated process by a multifunctional team of people who work together at the same location within our center. We have several such integrated teams, with each team dedicated to a particular region of the country or to a major customer account.

"Each team is responsible for the total end-to-end customer service process and serves as a single point of contact for our call-in customers. The good part is that everyone on a team is aware of the whole process and is being cross-trained in a variety of team jobs. Furthermore, any team member should be able to help a customer in a fraction of the time as compared to the old way.

In concluding her remarks, Diane admits, "While I think this change will make a great difference, I and the other managers of the customer service center are getting lots of complaints from the staff. For example, I have one person who refuses to cross-train two others on her job. Another associate is threatening to quit if he's forced to leave his old team to join a new multifunctional team.

"I just don't get it. Maybe our employees just don't have the ability to work in this new environment."

Case Analysis

There is a natural human tendency to resist any change that requires us to act and think in a dramatically new and different way. During such times, people are asked to give up the things that they are most proud of, such as hard-earned skills, valued relationships, tried and true approaches, and personally discovered secrets of success.

Letting go of the past and moving into the future, especially an uncertain future, is fraught with anxiety and insecurity. Major change brings with it the possibility of less authority, money, status, prestige, control, and even the risk of job failure and job loss.

During a time of transition in the workplace, employees deserve support, understanding, communication, and assurance that the new change will likely bring them greater benefits. Such support is especially important if an organization has a history of going through "flavor of the month" changes or failed attempts at improvement.

Action Tools

To effectively manage change, consider the following action tools:

 Provide a communication forum in which employees can openly express their fears and objections about an upcoming change. During this session, listen nonjudgmentally to your employees and express genuine appreciation for their honesty. You may hear points of resistance that can be dealt with easily, while other points might become the basis for some alterations in the planned change.

* Provide emotional support to employees who are forced to make work changes from safe, secure, and satisfying situations and relationships. Such employees experience emotions similar to those of personal loss and mourning. These include shock, denial, confusion, anger, blame, sadness, and depression. Through your empathy and understanding, you can help employees move through the difficult period and gain acceptance of needed change.

* Sell the change by clearly communicating the superior benefits of the new system or approach. These may include improvements in productivity, quality, market share, competitiveness, or overall profitability.

* Motivate employees to participate in planned change by recognizing them to the rest of the organization for their past successes and achievements and for their potential to help move the process forward. In addition, celebrate early successes and recognize contributing employees and teams.

* To encourage appropriate risk-taking, provide employees with a "safety net" for reasonable mistakes and failures and help them quickly recover through management support and employee training.

* Include your employees as fully and as early as possible in the change process. This way, you gain not only their best ideas but their personal support for the change. This belief is summarized in the "Principle of Ownership:"

> *What people are involved in helping to create, they own. . . .*
>
> *What people own, they support and are committed to.*
>
> *What people are not involved in helping to create, they do not own. . . .*
>
> *What people do not own, they resist and may even sabotage.*

* Ensure that all organizational systems are in sync so that the intended change will progress smoothly.

Often, important changes fail to meet expectations due to a lack of management coordination and organizational support from outmoded programs within such areas as finance, marketing, human resources, research and development, manufacturing, materials management, or legal affairs.

Section IV

Communicating for Positive Results

21

Planning and Controlling the Communication Process

Case Problem: "Communication Mismanagement"

"So, Howard, how did the meeting with the Jarvis people go?" asked Marv, the controller.

"What meeting?" replied Howard, the credit manager, with surprise. "You didn't ask me to attend any meeting."

"Look, Howard," Marv replied, "I dropped a note on your desk Thursday afternoon, explaining that I couldn't make my appointment on Friday with Ron Jarvis at Jarvis Mills. I let him know you'd be taking my place. I put the note on your desk myself."

"Oh, you mean that note under my telephone?" asked Howard. "Yes, I did get that, but I couldn't make out the message or who wrote it. The handwriting was so unclear; I just disregarded it."

Angry and annoyed at Howard and himself for the mess-up, Marv decided to go over to the cafeteria to calm down while grabbing a bite to eat. As he was drinking his coffee, Marv spotted Kevin, an accounting clerk, passing by carrying a lunch tray.

"Hey, Kevin!" called out Marv. "Come over and join me for lunch."

As Kevin sat down with his boss, Marv started tapping his finger on the table angrily.

"Kevin, I've been getting several complaints from people about your work on the cash flow reports and the Phase III accounting work. I've warned you before about these things."

As Marv continued to admonish his employee, a number of people sitting near them grew quiet, staring at the duo. Embarrassed by his boss's loud condemnation and humiliated by Marv's public display, Kevin jumped up from his chair and rushed out of the cafeteria.

"What did I do?" thought Marv to himself. "That guy is crazy."

As Marv finished his lunch, Rita, the director of human resources, asked him to stop by the human resources office to discuss a matter.

"Marv, two months ago at a special staff meeting," Rita began as the two met in her office, "I gave all managers some important employee forms to be filled out and returned to me immediately. It's now three weeks after the deadline. Where are the forms? And why don't you respond to my memos? I sent you three follow-ups to get these forms."

"Gee, Rita," reacted Marv, "I really don't know what to say. I recall the meeting and something about some personnel forms. But the night before, I had attended a late social function and was exhausted during your meeting. I guess the forms are around somewhere."

"But why didn't you answer my memos?" probed Rita further.

"Well, the fact is, I was going to," admitted Marv, "but I wasn't really sure what you wanted."

As Marv returned to his office, he overheard Judy, the accounting department secretary, comment to a supplier on the phone.

"Yes, Mr. Goodwin," Judy said, "Lacy will definitely call you early next week. I know how important that financial report is to you."

"What's going on?" interrupted Marv. "Where's Lacy? I gave her last Monday off, not the entire week!"

"That's strange," replied Judy. "Lacy told me you gave her the whole week off. And because of your suggestion, she was going to Jamaica with her boyfriend."

"You've got to be kidding," said Marv, annoyed. "Last week she asked for Monday off. I felt she had taken enough private time already and sarcastically told her, 'Why not take the entire week off and go to Jamaica with your boyfriend.'"

"Well, sir, I guess she took your advice and did just that," said Judy, laughing.

"Just another typical day," thought Marv. "Nothing ever seems to go right around here. Well, what can I expect with a staff like mine?"

Suddenly, Marv's thoughts were interrupted by a phone call from Jack, the general manager.

"Marv, I'm glad I got you in," said Jack. "What did you think of my proposal at yesterday's meeting to redesign the floor plan for the accounting department?"

Though knowing that Jack's plan would slow down the work flow, Marv praised the idea to Jack for fear that criticism of his boss's idea would be mistaken for disloyalty to management.

"Thanks, Marv," said Jack. "If there were any holes in my plan, I knew I could trust you to be frank about it with me."

Later that afternoon, as Marv looked at his watch at 4:50 PM, he remembered that he had to tell his staff about management's decision to consider closing down three plants and having to possibly lay off some 1,200 people. He was able to round up five of his seven managers and quickly convey this message. The staff listened to their boss's news and looked at each other in amazement.

"This decision may or may not affect us," Marv continued. "But either way, I would appreciate your telling the others who couldn't make this meeting."

At 5:00 PM, Judy rushed into the office.

"Your wife is waiting outside for you, Marv," she said. "Remember, your plane is leaving for Miami at 6:30 PM. I hope you have a good business trip and we'll see you next Wednesday back in the office."

With that, Marv ended the meeting abruptly, with the staff looking on in shock. As Marv rushed from the room, bidding them goodbye, the managers grew anxious about the possible layoffs.

Case Analysis

The vast majority of mistakes made in business are due to breakdowns in the communication process. Because of this fact and because managers are responsible for managing departmental communication activities, it is imperative that they understand and are able to manage the process.

Communication breakdown is a major problem in every situation in the case presented above. Marv, the controller, is the key violator of the communication principles vital to effective management.

First, it is apparent that Howard's failure to meet with Ron Jarvis at Jarvis Mills was due to Marv's poor choice of a communication medium—the memo—to convey his urgent request and also to his sloppy and illegible handwriting which was unintelligible to Howard.

Second, it is evident from the embarrassing encounter with Kevin in the cafeteria that Marv chose both the wrong place—a public cafeteria—and the wrong time—immediately following the blow-up with Howard, with his temper still hot—to discipline an employee.

Third, why didn't Marv fulfill his obligation to provide Rita, the human resources director, with those important employee forms? Marv may have attended her meeting, but he was absent mentally due to his late social function the night before. Had Marv recognized his own exhaustion on the day of the meeting, he could have brought along a more alert associate to listen and take notes of important business.

Furthermore, there is no excuse for Marv's failure to respond to Rita's follow-up requests for the employee forms. If he didn't know what she wanted specifically, a quick visit to her office would have resolved that problem. Not reacting to urgent solicitations by colleagues is a flagrant violation of effective team communication.

Fourth, Marv's inappropriate "sarcasm" in telling Lacy she could not have Monday off by jokingly advising her to go to Jamaica for the week was taken literally. In serious business communication, sarcasm—that is, saying one thing, but meaning just the opposite—should not be used. Misinterpretation and hurt feelings could result. As Marv learned, if one has something to say, it must be stated directly ("No, you've had sufficient personal vacation time this year.").

Fifth, one of Marv's worst communication failures was to lie to Jack, his manager, about the virtue of Jack's floor plans for the accounting department. To protect himself and how he might be viewed by management, Marv chose to praise, rather than criticize, the plans.

Finally, Marv's lack of planning on how and when to communicate the possible layoff decision to his people caused a great deal of anxiety and created many false beliefs and rumors over the next few days.

Action Tools

To minimize communication breakdown and maximize positive results, the following tips can be helpful:

* Organize your message clearly in your mind before communicating it.
* Be sensitive to the feelings and reactions of the receiver when sending messages.
* Choose the time and place for the communication based on the nature of the message (i.e., positive or negative) and the time available for both the manager and the receiver to fully discuss the message.
* Choose the appropriate medium carefully—face-to-face, written, e-mail, or telephone—for the particular message. For example, one does not convey an urgent action request by letter or memo sent through conventional postal or interoffice systems. Such a message can be more quickly conveyed face-to-face, by telephone, by e-mail, or by fax.
* Be results-oriented and aware of how your communication may achieve your goal. Every message conveyed is linked to a result.
* Respond appropriately to messages received; this is just as important a responsibility as sending effective communications.

22

Communicating Honestly and Directly

Case Problem: "The Snoopervisor"

"Larry, I don't believe our manager," complained Dorothy, a senior chemist, to a colleague. "She didn't believe that I was at the West Coast conference giving a speech on analytical chemistry. It's absolutely insulting."

"What's going on?" asked Larry.

"After returning from the national meeting in San Diego," explained Dorothy, "I put together a brief memo describing my presentation, sent it to Alice, our manager, and asked that she insert it into my employee file to add to my record of professional accomplishments.

"Yesterday, I was informed by another chemist that Alice had been checking up on me. She was going around asking if I had actually attended the conference and given my presentation."

"Dorothy, a month ago, Alice did something similar to me," Larry said. "At a weekly staff meeting, I mentioned my participation on a project of the local chapter of The Chemists Society.

"Alice didn't acknowledge my comments during that meeting. But the following week, I learned from others on the staff that she was questioning the project's value and even viewing it as wasted time."

"You know, Larry," Dorothy continued, "the more I think about it, the worse it gets. Alice should be acknowledging our hard work and professional involvements, not going behind our backs, questioning our honesty and discounting our efforts."

Case Analysis

Frustration and resentment will occur if a manager doesn't communicate openly and directly with staff. Here, the manager has set up communication barriers by going behind the backs of employees as a "snoopervisor," questioning employee accomplishments and discounting staff initiatives.

If Alice had specific questions about staff activities, she should have asked her employees directly. Her lack of honest and direct communication pertaining to the staff's professional accomplishments led to serious morale problems.

Action Tools

To effectively communicate as a manager, consider the following action tools:

- ✳ Recognize that individuals want a leader they can trust.
- ✳ Use a direct and honest communication approach with staff.
- ✳ Deal directly with employees, rather than sidestepping issues of importance to them.
- ✳ Develop the image of an honest and open communicator—one who does not have to resort to underhanded tactics and behind-the-scenes gossip.

23

Maintaining Open Communication Channels

Case Problem: "Kept in the Dark"

Hans, the company's quality control manager, was talking with Kate, an inventory control specialist.

"Kate, I heard your boss, Joe, got a new job with our biggest competitor," said Hans.

"That's impossible," Kate exclaimed. "I was just talking with him the other day and he mentioned nothing about this."

"I could have sworn that you knew," responded Hans. "Weren't you supposed to be next in line for Joe's job of inventory manager? And didn't you tell me you had a career plan supported by Joe, as well as by Art, the vice president?"

"Yes," replied Kate. "When Joe got his promotion, I was to move into his spot."

"More bad news, Kate," continued Hans. "Joe has already been replaced by some new guy from Oklahoma."

"Hold on!" interrupted Kate. "Are you saying I was passed over for the manager's spot by some outsider without any consideration or prior notification?"

"Gee, Kate, I didn't mean to be the bearer of bad news," said Hans. "I just assumed you were in on things."

"In on things?" asked Kate incredulously. "It seems management has kept me in the dark on purpose and never intended to keep its part of our career plan bargain. And after I've given this company six years of loyal service!"

"Kate, it sounds as if you had better see Art immediately and find out what is happening," advised Hans.

"Oh, and I guess you want me to introduce myself to the new inventory manager and offer him my undying service," retorted Kate. "No way! I'll do my job, but you can bet that greenhorn won't get any extra effort from me!"

Case Analysis

In the past, Kate's working relationships with her superiors were characterized by open, honest communication and trust. She believed that any important information that concerned her job and career would be readily supplied. If the shocking news she heard through the grapevine is true, Kate's feelings of anger are justified.

Whatever the reason for this "information blackout," management is guilty of concealing vital information from an important and trusting employee who is directly affected. But, if Kate—out of anger or resentment—fails to confirm the facts directly with the vice president, she is equally guilty of setting up barriers.

Action Tools

To exhibit an open and honest communication style, consider the following action tools:

* Keep communication channels open with employees, particularly on matters that directly affect their jobs, security, and careers.
* Develop and maintain trust in your management-employee relationships by continually sharing as much business information as possible, regardless of whether you believe it will be received positively or negatively.
* Do not risk destroying your credibility and building barriers with employees by selectively communicating only that information you wish to share. In positive and trusting work relationships, employees appreciate being kept informed about their work, careers, and business.

24

Using Nonverbal Communications Effectively

Case Problem: "More Than Words Can Say"

Linda, manager of technical services, and Marty, manager of human resources, were chatting over lunch in the company cafeteria.

"Marty, I just don't think senior management in this company really cares about anything around here," complained Linda.

"Why do you say that?" asked Marty.

"Well, the other day, when I went to the general manager's office with a great new idea," replied Linda, "Carl invited me in to sit down and explain it to him."

"What's wrong with that Linda?" questioned Marty.

"It was what happened during that meeting that drove me up the wall!" exclaimed Linda. "The guy didn't even close the door to his office and, within two minutes, took a call that could have been handled later on. Don't you think that calls should be held until later if a meeting is important enough?"

"Yes, I suppose they should," replied Marty. "And he could have closed his door, too. What else did he do?"

"While I was speaking," continued Linda, "he kept fidgeting with his pen, looking around the room, and rolling his eyes as if to say, 'What a bunch of bull.' You know, Marty, after about ten minutes, when he told me my idea was pretty good and we should talk about it again sometime, I was really relieved to get out of that office.

"Do you think the boss is interested in my idea? I sure got mixed signals in that meeting. If I had to choose, I would say the guy is totally turned off."

"Well, something is going on," responded Marty. "On one hand, the boss invites you in to his office to talk to you. Then ten minutes later, he tells you it's a good idea and wants to talk about it again. On the other hand, he seems to be showing a lack of interest by his expressions and actions. However Carl feels about your idea, he definitely seems to be sending two different messages that should be sorted out immediately."

"Marty, are you suggesting that I go back to Carl and level with him about my feelings?" asked Linda.

"Absolutely," said Marty. "You have to know his feelings up front or you could waste a lot of time in developing that proposal."

Case Analysis

Marty seems to be aware of the importance that nonverbal communication plays in a meeting and of the confusion that can result from mixed signals. The fidgeting, eye rolling, and phone answering would appear to suggest a negative attitude and lack of interest. However, inviting Linda in to the general manager's office and making a positive comment about the proposal would suggest just the opposite. What is the truth? The suggestion for Linda to go back to her manager and express her confusion, seeking to understand his true attitude, is a good one.

Action Tools

Enhance your communication effectiveness by considering the following nonverbal communication tips:

 Make sure your nonverbal signals or body language support and complement your verbal message. Be as clear as possible and avoid any confusion that may be created by lax body language.

★ When listening to employees, show that you are genuinely interested by being attentive and putting aside other matters and concerns. If you are honestly preoccupied with other urgent issues, level with your employees and reschedule your meetings.

★ As a listener, if you are confused because a speaker's verbal message and nonverbal signals are in conflict, state your confusion and seek clarification.

25

Speaking Techniques for Management Presentations

Case Problem: "The Turn-Off Speaker"

"This guy has got to be kidding," thought Rob, a senior analyst who was attending his manager's talk at a dinner meeting of the Chamber of Commerce.

Sam, the manager of financial planning, had been asked to speak two months ago about the importance of the financial presentation when dealing with top management.

As Sam spoke, Rob strained to hear Sam's words, which were muttered in a very low volume.

"I wish he'd look up at the audience at least once in a while," thought Rob, "and appear somewhat interested in what he's saying. He's just reading that stupid speech as if he'd never seen it before."

Just then, a sudden loud, deep noise pierced Rob's left ear—the president of a local restaurant chain began snoring, with his head fallen backward. Three people at the side of the room became engaged in a personal conversation. And two individuals from the front of the room got up and walked out.

"How utterly embarrassing for Sam," thought Rob. "And also what a humiliation for our company."

At that point, Sam's words brought joy to Rob's ears and a sigh of relief to the business people present.

"Well, I guess I've run out of time now," Sam told the audience. "In fact, I suppose I've gone over my allotted time by about twenty minutes. I'd like to now turn the program back to Barbara."

After these final remarks, Barbara, the Chamber official, stood up and thanked Sam for his views.

"I had hoped that we would be able to have a question-and-answer session with Sam," she added, "but our time has run out."

Case Analysis

How could Sam, the financial planning manager, have embarrassed his employee, his company and himself in this way? How could he have been so unprepared and unpolished in delivering his talk to this important community group?

Sam assumed that presenting before groups was simply a matter of reading out loud. After agreeing to speak at the dinner meeting two months ago, he had Mary Jo, a member of the financial staff, write his speech for him. The day before the speech, he received the manuscript from Mary Jo. Sam assumed that she had done her job earnestly and, consequently, felt it was unnecessary to review the speech for content and accuracy.

In addition, he failed to rehearse it—that is, practice it out loud several times under timed conditions. As a result, he could not communicate with feeling and understanding because he was unfamiliar with the talk's content.

When Sam asked Rob to attend the talk, Rob thanked his manager for the opportunity and offered to serve as a trial audience for a run-through and critique. But Sam refused, shrugging off such practice as unnecessary.

Action Tools

The speech presentation is an important vehicle for creating a favorable image and positive visibility for the manager, department, and company. To help ensure the success of your management presentations, consider the following action tools:

★ Understand the audience, the specific purpose of the talk, the time schedule allotted, and the need to make a favorable impression.

★ Make certain the content of the talk is well-organized and helps the speaker achieve the goal.

★ Rehearse the presentation before one or more individuals willing to give honest and helpful criticism.

★ Look at the audience as much as possible while delivering the talk.

★ Speak up and project your voice so that everyone in the audience can hear easily.

★ Speak with understanding and expression.

★ Keep the talk moving, well-paced, and within the time allotted. This will allow time for questions and answers and help create a positive impression.

26

Using the Written Medium Effectively

Case Problem: "Put It in Writing"

It had been three months since his promotion from product engineer to manager of product development, and Don was nervous about his meeting with Jack, vice president of research and development. Although this was to be his first informal review, it was important to Don.

Jack arrived in Don's office, and Don greeted him warmly. After some conversation about business in general, the two began to discuss Don's progress as the manager of product development.

"Jack, you know how important this job is to me, and I've tried hard to take control of the department since Janet left," Don began. "But I'll be honest with you: There just doesn't seem to be enough time in the day, and the staff is always arguing about this and that."

"What do you mean?" asked Jack. "How is your time being wasted, and what is everyone arguing about?"

"Well, it's like this," replied Don. "I never thought meetings were that important before, but now I see that you really can't run a department without regular and frequent meetings. In fact, I have several staff meetings each week. And that's just it. They're so time consuming."

"What's the purpose of these meetings?" inquired Jack.

"Well, you know, to keep the staff informed about company matters and to let them all know my feelings, opinions, and positions on things," replied Don. "They've got to understand the rules and management's position. Don't you agree?"

"I wonder," reacted Jack. "Perhaps you're holding too many meetings. Is it possible that much of what you're saying in your meetings could be communicated by e-mail or interoffice correspondence?

"You see, Don, staff meetings are very important for many things, but I have found that much of what is said in meetings—which, by the way, require everyone's presence—might better be put in writing. Then you and the staff would have written records of the information conveyed and be able to save meeting time, too."

"Maybe that's it, Jack," said Don. "I think you've put your finger on it. I'm a great talker, but I hate to write. I'll bet I could save at least half the meeting time by putting my thoughts in writing.

"And I think now I know the reason for so many arguments. Not once since I started this job did I put a single job assignment in writing. All assignments have been handled face to face but with no follow-up memos. We simply have no record of our job discussions, and this constantly causes misunderstandings and arguments later."

"I see your point," agreed Jack. "Putting your ideas in writing certainly has its benefits. Perhaps both of us could work on writing up some procedures for research and development. You know, written operating procedures could save a lot of time in explaining over and over again the same routines to various people at different times. These written procedures would also help prevent arguments over who does what, where and when."

Case Analysis

In this situation, Don, a new product development manager, struggles in his new position. The informal performance discussion that he has with Jack, the vice president, helps bring out two of Don's greatest frustrations: too much time wasted and too many arguments in the department.

With the vice president's help, Don realizes that considerable staff meeting time could be saved by putting much of the information he has for his people in writing. In addition, both men come to realize that time is wasted and arguments are caused because job assignments and basic work procedures have not been documented in writing to serve as guides and references for follow-up and future action.

Action Tools

To effectively use the written medium, consider these tips:

✦ Put information that does not require immediate discussion in writing to save staff meeting time.

✦ Put information in writing to provide a permanent record and documentation of discussions, events, or directives for employees' future reference and guidance.

✦ Put information in writing to prevent misunderstanding, arguments, and wasted time in the execution of job duties.

27

Listening Effectively to Employees

Case Problem: "Hear Ye, Hear Ye!"

Very upset about a recent conversation with his manager, the employee benefits manager, Jim, complained to his colleague, Carol.

"Carol, I dread speaking with that guy. He's so insulting."

"What happened?" asked Carol.

"Well, I made an appointment with Ron, our beloved manager," replied Jim, "to get some ideas on how to handle the Burns Insurance Company project. I went into his office and, as usual, he kept the door open. It was like Grand Central Station, with people tramping in and out.

"It was very distracting, Carol; the meeting was a complete waste. He was answering the phone and talking to me at the same time, bragging about how he could conduct two discussions at once. But even though he was nodding and agreeing with me, he seemed a million miles away."

"He was probably more concerned about the bowling tournament he's in tonight," responded Carol. "He's acted like that with me, too; so I've long since stopped going to him for his thoughts on projects. It simply isn't worth it.

"Not only does Ron seem bored with me, he's actually told me that my 'monotone voice' puts him to sleep. He even had the nerve to tell me I had a speech impediment! And two months ago, during an important meeting, I couldn't keep him on the subject. The only thing he was interested in was commenting on my dress.

"There's just no talking with that guy. He simply doesn't listen."

Case Analysis

A critical part of the communication process is the ability to listen effectively. Ron, the employee benefits manager, has failed at this essential task, alienating the staff through his disregard for their time, energy, and efforts.

It is apparent from the conversation between these staff members that Ron places greater importance on his own thoughts and business than on the thoughts and business of his people. This is an unfortunate state of affairs, since the problems, needs, and thoughts of staff should be a manager's primary concern. Because Ron has lost the respect of his staff, his effectiveness as a manager has been seriously impaired.

Action Tools

To listen effectively to employees, consider the following action tools:

- ✳ Set aside all preoccupations and concerns with other matters, turning your full attention to the discussion and the person with whom you are speaking.
- ✳ Concentrate on what the speaker is saying. Do not be distracted by or criticize the speaker's voice, dress, or mannerisms.
- ✳ Do not waste the speaker's time by shifting the direction of the conversation to your own interests and needs.
- ✳ Organize the communication setting for minimum distraction and maximum privacy and attention. This includes considering holding all calls and visitors.

28

Managing for Customer Satisfaction

Case Problem: "Get to the End of the Line!"

It is that time of year again. College recruiters from major corporations are visiting campuses across the nation in search of fresh talent. Ann and Tom, recruiters from a leading West Coast computer maker, are in New York City for ten days. They will meet with graduating seniors at universities in and around the metropolitan area.

Staying at a midtown Manhattan hotel, Ann and Tom rent their automobile from We Care Rent-a-Car, located across the street from the hotel. They rent the car for ten days at the corporate rate of $66 a day. But where can they park the car in the evening?

They learn that We Care has a new service that can save them money on parking and offers convenience as well. For only $8 a night, instead of the usual $24 a night at many public garages, We Care customers can park their rental cars at the We Care Rent-a-Car garage. This seems like a good deal, and the two recruiters decide to park in the We Care garage each night.

On Monday evening, following their first day of recruiting, Ann and Tom return to the City and park at We Care's garage across from the hotel. They drive in, drop their car, receive a parking stub from the car attendant, and are told to pay $8 the following morning to pick up their car.

On the following day, Ann and Tom walk into the Rent-a-Car store and ask a counter attendant where they can pay their $8 to pick up their parked car. They are told gruffly by the attendant, "Can't you see the line? You'll have to get to the end of the line and wait like everyone else."

The line is long and winding, and the two recruiters are confused.

"But, ma'am," says Ann, "This is the car rental line. We're just trying to pick up our parked car that we rented from We Care and pay our $8."

"This line is for both car rental and car parking," says the attendant, annoyed. "You'll just have to get to the end of the line like everyone else and wait your turn."

Twenty minutes later, Ann and Tom walk up to the counter and pay their $8. They are upset, having had to wait a long time in the store counter line.

Upon parking their car Tuesday evening, Ann and Tom speak with the night manager. They explain that they had rented a We Care car for ten days and needed to park their car each night, adding that that morning they had to wait in the car rental line for twenty minutes just to get their parked car.

"We Care Rent-a-Car has just expanded its service to include public parking," the night manager explains, "but this new service is also provided by our car rental people. Unfortunately, this means that parking customers have to stand in the same line as the new rental customers each morning. I'm sorry for the inconvenience."

"In that case, we will need to park elsewhere," says Ann. "We can't waste our time each morning standing in long lines just to get our parked car."

"Look, although I'm not supposed to do this, I guess I could help you guys out," offers the night manager. "When you bring your car back each evening, go to the counter inside, prepay the $8 charge, and I'll approve the prepayment. Then, each morning, simply give your prepaid ticket to the garage attendant, and you'll immediately receive your car. How's that?"

The recruiters are happy with the night manager's solution and thank him for his concern. Over the next several days, everything goes as planned and the recruiters receive their car each morning with no delay.

Then, on the eighth morning, as they hand their prepaid stub to the garage attendant, a man walks up to them, introducing himself as the general manager of the We Care facility.

"We seem to have a problem here," he states. "Our records regarding your parked car are all messed up. Somehow you've been prepaying your parking fee each night instead of in the mornings like everyone else. Is that right?"

"Yes," the two respond, happily. "And we really appreciate that your night manager helped us avoid the long lines in the mornings."

"Oh, really!" exclaims the general manager. "He's not supposed to do that. He broke the rules by letting you pay early. You people should be paying your fee each morning like everyone else. I'm going to have to write him up for not following procedure."

Not believing their ears at the general manager's harsh reaction to his night manager's helpfulness, the two recruiters appeal.

"Don't get that nice man into trouble," they plead. "If he hadn't helped us out, we would have parked elsewhere."

"The night manager should know better," responds the general manager as he walks away from the couple. "When he does things like this, the accountants get all confused, and I get the blame. No, he can't get away with this anymore. And you people will have to pay each morning like everyone else."

Case Analysis

We Care Rent-a-Car should probably be called We Care Less Rent-a-Car. Clearly this is a business where negative actions speak louder than positive words. There is no question that We Care has a good new business idea of expanding its current car rental business to include public parking at the same garage site. This idea creates a "win-win" situation for both We Care and its customers. For We Care, public parking is a potentially profitable new service. For We Care car rental customers, the benefits include parking convenience and reduced parking fees.

As is seen all too often in business, there is a clear breakdown here between the marketing and operations functions of We Care Rent-a-Car. The name of the company communicates the message: "We value our customers." In addition, the customer convenience and reduced parking prices for rental customers communicate that message as well.

Unfortunately, management has done little to plan and execute internal customer-oriented programs and procedures to support its marketing efforts. The counter attendant, for example, rudely orders the two customers to get to the end of the line, thus creating a very poor impression on even the most forgiving of customers. What's worse is the general manager's display of serious management shortcomings, including:

- Failure to plan and adapt internal systems—both counter and administrative services—for swift and pleasant customer handling
- Failure to recognize a talented night manager for his excellent problem-solving initiatives and ideas, as well as for his thoughtful customer service efforts
- Failure to treat customers with courtesy and respect
- Failure to orient and train staff in basic customer relations
- Failure to encourage continuous improvement and customer feedback
- Accusing, blaming, and reporting an enthusiastic manager for breaking rules and causing trouble, in spite of the individual's obvious success in keeping customers

Action Tools

The first and foremost commitment of the most successful businesses is unsurpassed customer care and service. Whether dealing with outside consumers or internal departments, this overriding principle must be demonstrated daily in every way possible.

Unfortunately, lack of total employee customer focus, coupled with failure to develop an integrated organization-wide approach, often leads to unnecessary customer frustration and vast numbers of lost customers each year.

To help create a true customer-friendly business environment, consider implementing the following action tools:

- Share your vision for customer care and satisfaction with all associates, emphasizing its great importance as a key competitive strategy.
- Clarify that the organization's quest for superior customer satisfaction should encourage employees to continuously seek new and improved ways for caring about and keeping customers.

✦ Get your customer message out often—at weekly meetings, in company newsletters, and during regular employee planning, feedback, and coaching sessions.

✦ Recognize and reward those employees who clearly demonstrate customer care.

✦ Work closely with other managers and carefully coordinate your customer satisfaction initiatives and programs.

✦ Lead by example in demonstrating your own personal concern about the critical role of customer care.

29

Writing Techniques for Successful Managers

Case Problem: "The Impressive Report"

"Well, what do you think?" inquired Ron, vice president of materials management, of his friend, Sam, vice president of sales and marketing. "An impressive report?"

"Honestly?" retorted Sam. "Do you want the honest-to-goodness truth?"

"Sure, this is an important proposal to be reviewed by the president," explained Ron. "We need the resources I'm requesting. My people are depending upon my ability to state our case clearly and forcefully to get the results we need."

"Okay, then, I'll level with you, Ron," asserted Sam. "Your report just doesn't make it. In fact, I'm not sure the president would understand what you're asking for and why. Your writing is too ambiguous and your language too stuffy."

"Go on," urged Ron. "I can handle it."

"Now, I'm no expert on communication," advised Sam, "but I don't think this twenty-page report will be read. It's just too lengthy. I bet you could cut it down to less than five pages and say the same thing."

"In other words, I'm being wordy and long-winded in my writing. Is that right?" inquired Ron.

"Exactly," replied Sam, "Keep it as brief as possible. And one more point. The attitude you've conveyed here seems harsh. If you want the president to approve more resources for your area, I don't think that scaring him into releasing funds is the best way to accomplish that goal. Threats, sarcasm, and curtness just won't work here."

"I suppose I could be more tactful, positive, and constructive," agreed Ron.

Case Analysis

In this situation, we see Sam, a good friend to Ron, giving honest feedback on Ron's senior management proposal. As Sam points out key writing problems, Ron accepts his friend's criticism and seeks to find ways to improve.

Unlike Ron, however, many of us have a tendency to defend life-learned writing skills that we believe have made us so effective in school and business. Typical defensive comments that are heard in the face of criticisms of our writing are: "In school you learn to play the game, and the game of writing is the more verbiage, the better" and "At work there is a standard written language style that everyone has always used. Why should I be any different?"

Impressive writing, however, does not result from lengthy, wordy or formal jargon, but rather from clear, natural, concise, and constructive communication.

Action Tools

To strengthen your business writing skills, consider the following suggestions:

✦ *Write concisely.* Conciseness is saying what has to be said in the fewest words possible without sacrificing completeness of thought or courtesy. Here, for example, is an unnecessarily wordy sentence: "Let me take this opportunity to say that your consideration relative to this proposal is absolutely essential." Rewritten more concisely, the sentence could read: "Please consider this proposal seriously."

✦ *Write clearly.* Clear writing is crisp, concrete, and natural, allowing the reader to immediately grasp the message. Here is an example of an unclear sentence that is ambiguous and confusing: "I will endeavor to ascertain the best arrangement and get back in touch." Rewritten more clearly, the sentence could read: "I will contact you Wednesday with my decision on your RT-112 proposal."

★ *Write courteously and constructively.* Courteous and constructive writing conveys feelings of consideration for the reader and interest in solutions rather than complaints. Here is an example of writing that offends and discounts the reader's feelings: "You have failed to support my department's efforts, and caused a great deal of wastefulness in this company." Rewritten with a better tone, the sentence could read: "Today, with top management support, we have a genuine opportunity to improve profitability through professional materials management practices."

30

Keeping Meetings on Track

Case Problem: "Curing Hidden Agenda-itis"

"Look, you've had more than enough time," exclaimed Marla, the director of planning, to Bob, the manager of production control. "I put you in charge of this committee so you could get everyone's idea and generate some intelligent solutions."

"I wasn't able to get past the first point on the agenda," replied Bob. "I tried, but it felt like I was on a treadmill. I just couldn't get the staff to come to any decisions.

"Mike kept telling the group our ideas would never fly. He said he's tried them all before. Barbara put down every suggestion I made and made me look like a fool. Sam just sat there like a dummy and never said anything at all. And Jeff only talked about the upcoming baseball game.

"It was a rough afternoon, Marla. Everyone seemed to be working at odds with each other."

Case Analysis

What Bob experienced in his meeting was a classic case of "hidden agenda-itis." This problem occurred because his official meeting goal—the public agenda—was blocked by Mike, Barbara, Sam, and Jeff, who pursued their own counterproductive personal goals—the hidden agenda.

People often use meetings such as Bob's to satisfy their own needs at the expense of others. As Bob realized from his frustrating session, hidden agenda-itis can be a major deterrent to effective meetings.

Mike hindered the group's progress by using "killer phrases" such as "It will never work," "We've tried that before," and "It won't hold water." Such phrases squelch individual thinking and healthy interaction. Mike's hidden agenda may have been to block the success of Bob's committee because of Mike's own past failures to sell the company on improvements he had recommended.

Barbara's personal put-downs suggest possible hostility directed toward Bob, either as a group leader or an individual. Such a meeting would, of course, provide Barbara with the perfect platform from which to launch a personal attack against Bob and publicly discredit him.

And Sam sits there, never saying anything. Is Bob aware that Sam was passed over twice for a promotion and may now feel disappointed and indifferent toward the business?

Finally, there's Jeff. He's very intelligent and could, if he wanted to, contribute a great deal to the group's work. The only problem is his social and recreational pursuits outweigh his professional interests these days. So, it's not surprising that he would use Bob's meeting to discuss sports.

An awareness of the hidden agenda individuals bring to a meeting—be it a one-on-one or a group of ten—can help a group leader better understand the group's dynamics and more intelligently control the group session.

Action Tools

To run effective meetings, a manager must be aware that individuals can bring destructive hidden agenda along with them, which often undermine the official meeting goals. To deal with this condition of "hidden agenda-itis" in meetings, the manager should follow these directions:

✴ Clearly outline, in writing, the official meeting agenda, emphasizing the importance of full group participation.

✴ Prevent "hidden agenda-itis" by leveling with individuals you suspect may use your meeting for their own purposes.

✴ Encourage all participants to contribute to the meeting agenda and stick to the schedule.

✴ Be prepared to tackle any hidden agenda that might surface. Remember, as a meeting leader, you are responsible for getting the group to achieve its goal. Awareness, tact, and strength are your tools in handling the problems that people bring to your meeting sessions.

Section V

Creating a Motivational Work Environment

31

Motivating Employees

Case Problem: "Motivate or Bust"

"Shooting the bull" over coffee, Kevin, the purchasing manager, and Jeff, his crony from manufacturing, were comparing "war stories" on how impossible it was for them to increase their workers' motivation.

"A bulldozer wouldn't move my people," insisted Kevin. "Why, I do everything for my people. If anything, Jeff, they have it too good around here.

"Just yesterday, I told one of my buyers, Rose, that she'd be taking on some new responsibilities around here and, of course, would be continuing to do her regular duties. I told her she would train a new person and attend, in my place, a few meetings with the 'big shots' upstairs. A great opportunity for her. The exposure, the opportunity to become involved in management—I thought she'd really go for it."

"Sounds great," Jeff agreed. "I'd jump at an opportunity like that."

"That's what I thought, too," agreed Kevin. "Those are the things I'd certainly be interested in. But Rose just turned red; she was actually steaming mad or something when she left my office. I just can't figure it out."

Case Analysis

This type of situation occurs when management believes it knows its employees' inner needs and drives without really knowing its employees at all on an individual basis.

Although Kevin was attempting to motivate Rose, the new

assignments were obviously perceived by her as undesirable, which was not Kevin's intention at all. Kevin believed that what was rewarding to him was also rewarding to others—an incorrect assumption, which quickly met with unpredicted, negative results.

Jeff is another member of management who assumes that what is right for him is also right for others. Together, Kevin and Jeff fuel each other's misconceptions about how to motivate their people correctly.

Action Tools

The key to motivating employees is knowing each person individually and not assuming that all people are alike or think just like you. To enhance your employee motivation skills, consider the following action tools:

- Meet with each person on your staff individually for approximately fifteen to twenty minutes. During these one-on-one meetings, get to know employees as individuals, listen caringly and learn what they really want and need in their jobs, careers, and lives. You will quickly realize from these one-on-one meetings that each person is different, with unique desires, frustrations, dreams, and hopes.
- With a knowledge of your employees' individual needs, try your best to intelligently and appropriately provide rewarding and meaningful assignments that they will approach with enthusiasm, drive, and pride. When job assignments help individuals satisfy important personal needs, people work harder and with greater pride to accomplish their job goals.
- Because these one-on-one motivational sessions are of great importance, try to establish a regular time each month to meet briefly with each of your employees. During these meetings, you have two key tasks. First, listen caringly and carefully for changing needs and frustrations. Second, be prepared to demonstrate flex-

ibility by either maintaining current assignments or adapting assignments to meet changing employee needs.

★ As a practical matter, you will not be able to satisfy all of your employees' needs all of the time. Your goal is to be attuned to your employees' feelings and to do your very best to help make each employee's work as personally meaningful and rewarding as possible. If you make this serious commitment to your employees, you and your organization will reap the benefits of improved motivation, morale, and productivity.

32

Fostering a Positive Work Environment

Case Problem: "A Gloomy Feeling"

"No, absolutely not," insisted Frank, the accounting manager, to Malinda, a staff accountant. "You've been here only six months and are still in training as far as I'm concerned. Before you start telling me my business, get some experience, keep your eyes and ears open, and your mouth shut!"

Shocked and annoyed at the accounting manager's reaction to her plan for improving the design of an accounting form, Malinda stormed out of Frank's office.

"I'll never again give that guy another idea for improving things around here," swore Malinda as she walked into her office.

"Well, what did Frank say?" asked Harry, a colleague, who had quietly entered Malinda's office. "I'll bet he didn't even listen."

"No, Harry, he did listen," said Malinda. "But right after I explained my plan, he became ugly and put me down for being too new on the job to have any helpful ideas."

"I told you so," gloated Harry. "The guy doesn't, and never did, care about anybody's opinion but his own. He thinks he's the big brain around here because he's the boss, and we're just a bunch of work horses.

"Just last week, I asked Frank to let me take charge of an important project with which I was familiar. All I wanted was the freedom to make some independent decisions without 'papa bear' approving everything at every step of the way. I got nowhere but, of course, I really didn't expect to. The guy just doesn't trust anyone."

"I can't accept that attitude," protested Malinda. "You've been here for seven years, and you're treated as badly as me. Why do you even stay around?"

"I need the job, so I generally maintain a low profile," explained Harry in a low voice. "But now and then, I feel a little cocky and try something crazy. It never works though. Nothing really changes around here. No real hope!"

As the two accountants spoke, they became aware of sobbing in the hallway outside Malinda's office. Ann, the accounting manager's secretary, was wiping her eyes when Malinda and Harry came up to inquire about what happened.

"Oh, you guys can figure it out," said Ann. "Mr. Big Heart, Frank, just put down my work. I give that creep my very best and even work three extra nights this week so he looks good at the management staff meeting. Now, when I expect some appreciation, he tells me it's my job to make him look good—whatever the cost. Then he turns around and turns down my request to attend my daughter's graduation next week."

As Malinda and Harry try to console Ann, all of a sudden, Frank, the accounting manager, jumps out from behind a wall.

"O.K., O.K.," he shouted, "the pity party is over! The three of you have bad attitude problems. You, Ann, you should be at your desk typing, not standing in the hall complaining. You, Harry, a senior staff member, I expected more from you. And Malinda, I'm warning you, don't question my ways!"

Case Analysis

Frank, the manager, has effectively created a negative work climate that saps the initiative, energy, and dignity from his staff. Hopelessness, neglect, and distrust dominate the work environment.

The net effect of Frank's negative tactics is a climate that discourages commitment, initiative, and innovation and instead breeds apathy, contempt, and even sabotage.

Action Tools

A manager is responsible for helping to create a positive motivational work climate for the staff. This important effort requires a trust in and respect for one's employees, a dedication to professional development, and a commitment to team productivity. The following actions will help develop such a climate:

* Favorably acknowledge initiatives, proposals, and any new ideas offered by members of the staff.
* Willingly delegate as much authority as possible to associates who want to make decisions in their own areas of responsibility.
* Seek out employee ideas and opinions when making decisions affecting the department.
* Provide positive recognition to employees performing well on the job.
* Express personal gratitude for extra efforts extended by members of the department.
* Always show sensitivity to your people's feelings by using common courtesies such as "Good morning," "Have a nice evening," "I'm sorry to hear about your trouble at home," "I hope you're feeling better today" or "Why don't you come in and we can talk about it?"

33

Cultivating Employee Initiative and Enthusiasm

Case Problem: "The Frivolous Project"

"Just forget it. It's out of the question!" shouted Gary, the vice president and publisher. "I want you to spend your time on high-payoff activities in technical development, not on some frivolous . . ."

"Gary, this is a project that's important to me," interrupted Mary, his editor-in-chief "I've been wanting to do this type of work for some time now. I think it's unfair of you to be like this. This project will have a long-term payback for the company and you."

"It's out of the question," repeated Gary. "No."

Mary broke out in a cold sweat as she became more and more angry at her boss of three months. She could only think of how hopeless her future would be to work for a boss like Gary, especially having worked for the past eight years for a former manager who welcomed her professional opinions and initiatives.

"Gary, you're wrong about this project," asserted Mary. "Let me have a shot at it, please. I will also handle all my current editorial responsibilities—nothing will suffer—I guarantee it!"

"That's not good enough," snapped Gary. "As I said, projects like this are a drain on company resources, and I won't have my employees doing anything that doesn't jibe with my plans. So that's the end of it. I don't want to hear any more about it!"

"Gary, I'm telling you, I'm totally disappointed," stated Mary. "I was hoping we'd be able to work well together, but if this is any indication of things to come, well, then I just don't know."

As Mary walked out of the boss's office, she thought of how much she would have enjoyed working on her project but now could only think of what an insensitive, narrow-minded boss she had.

Case Analysis

Here is a situation in which an executive could have built a win-win relationship between himself and a key member of his staff. Instead, Gary, the vice president, came in as the "heavy" and did not allow Mary the opportunity to work on a project of special importance to her. His attitude was that of a "know-it-all," allowing Mary no input into her own work plans.

Mary is a professional who had been a hard-working, enthusiastic individual. Now she feels stifled in her work as well as put off by her manager's inflexibility and seeming lack of concern for her professional interests.

Action Tools

Cultivate employee initiative and enthusiasm by following these suggestions:

- ✦ Listen to the thoughts and desires of your people and encourage their individual creative expression and contributions.
- ✦ Allow sufficient flexibility, independence, and freedom for your more accomplished and senior staff members so that they can pursue their job objectives in a self-directed manner. This positive attitude and respect toward your employees will be repaid in enhanced motivation and performance.
- ✦ Consider allowing employees time to pursue their own projects even though they may be somewhat peripheral to your immediate goals. As long as core business responsibilities are handled professionally, such consideration and flexibility will pay off in terms of heightened enthusiasm and employee appreciation.

34

Gaining the Trust of the Staff

Case Problem: "The Distrusted Manager"

While having lunch together, Tom, the director of the construction division of a consulting engineers firm, was expressing his frustration to a friend, Sol, the director of power engineering.

"I don't know, Sol. I just can't seem to whip up my staff and get them excited about anything these days."

"What's wrong?" inquired Sol, sympathetically.

"Well, do you recall that management study we were involved in several months ago?" asked Tom.

"Sure," replied Sol. "I believe its goal was to see how well our management team functioned. And as I recall, power engineering looked great in the results."

"I wish I could say the same for construction," lamented Tom. "I received a very low score on the variable of 'trust' from my project management staff. I just can't understand it. I've always supported my people's interests."

At that very moment, on the other side of the cafeteria, the construction project management staff were having lunch and talking.

"I'm just so burnt up about Tom," said one of the project managers. "That promotion he promised me last year—well, he just went ahead and gave the job to some guy from outside the company."

"Something similar happened to me," said another member of the staff. "Tom gave me his word that I would get a special assignment I've wanted for a long time now. But when I went to him last week to find out when I would be starting on it, he said he never gave his word on anything. What a liar!"

"Well, that figures," joined in another staff member. "For the last three months, I've been helping Tom out in training the new people on staff. As you know, all of that was on my own time. Tom said he wouldn't forget my assistance. Well, did he forget it! I was shocked at my raise this past month—one of the lowest ever. That's the thanks I get."

"The same thing happened to me," agreed another employee at the table. "Tom knew I was going on an extended vacation to China in October. In fact, several months before, he personally approved my taking three weeks together for that trip. October comes around, I'm ready for the trip, and Tom tells me he never approved anything. I had to cancel the entire vacation and lost $500 on the deal, too. Can you believe that?"

As the staff exchanged stories about their manager, Phil, a twenty-five-year veteran in the department, walked over to the table and showed the group the latest edition of the firm's magazine.

"So, Phil, where's the picture and article about your twenty-five-year recognition party?" asked someone from the group.

"It's not here," replied Phil. "I'm kind of upset. You know, Tom said he'd take the pictures we shot at the party and write up a release for this edition of the firm's magazine. Well, I guess it wasn't really important to him."

Case Analysis

A major ingredient of effective leadership is the concept of "trust." Employee trust of management is developed as a result of management deeds, not empty promises or forgotten intentions.

In this case, Tom, the director of construction, has a serious problem with group distrust. Because of his consistent failure to keep promises and follow up on commitments to employees, Tom's credibility is nonexistent.

Without trust in their manager's word, honor, or motives, the project management staff is unlikely to fully cooperate with Tom in his divisional efforts.

Action Tools

Develop a reputation for being a trustworthy manager by considering the following action tools:

* Make promises and commitments only when you intend to fulfill them.
* If you cannot realistically follow through on a commitment, be honest about it and try to work out some other arrangement, if possible.
* When you do make promises and commitments to others, follow through as quickly as possible. Avoid dragging your feet on needed action.
* Let your reputation for honesty precede you, and stand as a shining example for the employees you lead.

35

Exhibiting a Healthy Management Attitude

Case Problem: "The Right Management Attitude"

"So, Hilda, how's the job search going?" asked Larry, the sales promotion manager, to his gloomy colleague.

"Not too well," replied Hilda, who had made the decision two months earlier to start looking for a market research manager's job in another firm. "You know, Larry, I'm not too keen on having to look elsewhere for work, but I just can't take our beloved boss's negative attitude and critical manner any more."

"I wish you would reconsider staying," said Larry. "Just try to be like me: Avoid Ken as much as possible, and when he does put you down or say something stupid, try to ignore it."

"It's not that easy for me," claimed Hilda. "Although I may see him only 10 percent of the time, that short time is sufficient to ruin the rest of the week for me. His phony smile, caustic comments, and condescending attitude really annoy me.

"No, Larry, with Ken here in the driver's seat, there's no hope for people like me who want to get ahead and really do important things."

As the two colleagues were talking, Agnes, the president's secretary and a personal friend of Larry, walked into the marketing area.

"Listen, you guys," greeted Agnes. "Guess who just stepped down involuntarily and is going back to do some work as a brand manager? It's Ken—your boss! I just heard Mike, the president, advise him to give up the marketing vice president's job for the good of the company. . . . You know all the complaints and problems you folks have been having around here!

Well, Ken fought and argued about the president's request but finally gave in!"

"This is great news," cheered Larry. "Now, you don't have to leave, Hilda."

"Yes, this is good news, but Ken will still be on staff," replied Hilda.

"But Hilda," reasoned Agnes, "he won't have any authority over you or anyone anymore. Plus, I heard Mike tell Ken he would be replaced by Kathy. You get along well with her, don't you?"

"Now that's good news!" exclaimed Hilda, with a sigh of relief. "She's a great choice for marketing VP. Did you know that Kathy's positive attitude and support during the time I've been here is possibly the single greatest reason I've been able to survive under Ken's reign of terror?"

I think she's the perfect choice, too," agreed Larry. "Without her encouragement and help on several assignments, I don't think I could have made it either."

Later that day, the marketing staff was called in to a meeting at which time Mike, the president, announced that Ken would be stepping down for reasons of health and, instead, taking on a brand manager's job.

"Sure," thought Hilda and Larry, as they looked at each other, grinning.

When Mike announced Kathy as the new executive, the staff broke into applause, congratulating her.

Over the next three months, a small miracle occurred. Not only did Kathy eliminate all complaints and push marketing productivity up to an all-time high, but she also successfully converted Ken into one of her greatest supporters.

"See," said Hilda to Larry. "Kathy's positive attitude and encouraging approach even turned Ken around."

"You're right, Hilda," agreed Larry. "Even Ken, the ogre, needed a positive and supportive boss like Kathy to turn him into a positive force in the department.

"You've got it, Larry," echoed Hilda. "A key to the success of our department—especially with all the pressures we normally have in our work—was a manager with 'the right attitude.' "

Case Analysis

In this case, Ken's negative attitude had a highly destructive influence on his marketing staff. His distrust, condescending manner, and general negative behavior toward the staff caused a sense of department-wide depression. In addition, Ken's attitude forced a competent and experienced individual to stop trying and start searching for employment elsewhere.

Fortunately, though, the president recognized Ken's destructive impact on marketing and successfully saved the department by replacing Ken with Kathy, who was considered a natural leader and positive force by her colleagues.

Kathy's positive self-image, confidence in her colleagues, and supportive approach to individuals gave immediate relief to a situation no longer bearable by even the most tolerant employees. Clearly, a manager with the right management attitude can do more than imaginable to lift staff morale and performance.

Action Tools

To develop and display the right management attitude, consider the following action tools:

* Seek to demonstrate respect, concern, and good cheer to others as you go through your daily activities.
* Share with employees your positive expectations of them and your confidence in their abilities and dedication. Most people try hard to fulfill such favorable expectations when communicated to them by management.
* Praise freely and with gratitude when employees extend themselves and go the extra mile. Remember, noticing excellence in others and sharing genuine appreciation are special gifts possessed by the greatest leaders.

36

Creating a Healthy and Safe Working Environment

Case Problem: "The Soggy Ceiling"

"Look out, Sally," yelled Bob, an internal auditor, whose desk was next to hers. "Another piece of ceiling is about to fall on your desk!"

Just then, a six-inch piece of soggy ceiling plaster fell on Sally's desk, covering all her papers with dirty water and plaster.

"That's it, Bob," said Sally. "This ceiling has fallen for the last time. Last week, Mr. Simon, our assistant production superintendent, was sitting in that chair and was drenched when a piece of ceiling from under the second floor bathroom fell on him."

Overhearing Bob and Sally complaining about the soggy ceiling, Mel, another auditor in the office, joined in the conversation.

"Do you see this red nose?" he asked "Do you see these bloodshot eyes? Do you hear me sneezing over there? Do you know why I'm sick as a dog with this terrible cold? It's because there's no heat in this place. I brought a thermometer in today and it's 46 degrees in the office. We have no heat!"

Looking at their colleague, Sally and Bob agreed that the heating in the office was terrible during the winter, but they also remarked that summer months brought no relief because of a lack of air conditioning.

As the three colleagues commiserated over their working conditions, Connie, the department secretary, ran over to them with tears in her eyes.

"I can't stand it anymore," she said. "We work in a public corridor.

Every time anyone wants to go from the production area to the snack bar, they walk right through our office. And when they open the doors, the grinding and pounding of the equipment is deafening. We have no privacy, no peace, no quiet! I can't get anything done around here. I'm always being distracted."

Just then, Connie reached down to scratch her leg and saw a large roach jumping off her shoe.

As the staffers decried their poor working conditions, the boss walked up to them with a well-dressed young man and introduced him as a candidate for the new auditor's position. The manager asked each member of the staff to take a few minutes and tell the candidate about the benefits of working for this company.

Nodding approval to their boss, while glancing around at each other, the staff smilingly agreed to tell the candidate "everything they could" about working in the department.

Case Analysis

Safeguarding the health and safety of all employees is a vital management responsibility. Accordingly, managers are held accountable for implementing company health and safety policies and procedures within their respective areas.

Managers should be alert to unhealthy conditions that may cause illness and disease, and to unsafe equipment and facilities that may raise the likelihood of on-the-job injuries and accidents.

The protection of employee health and safety is a humane management endeavor, sound business practice, and serious legal obligation.

State laws and many local ordinances seek to ensure workplace health and safety. In addition, the Occupational Safety and Health Act (OSHA)—a comprehensive federal law—requires employers to provide a healthy and safe workplace for employees. Failure by managers to comply with these laws predisposes companies to legal claims and severe penalties.

In the case above, the department displayed a total lack of concern for its employees' health and safety. In addition, the hazardous working conditions and subhuman work environment seriously affected morale, productivity, and quality.

Action Tools

To help create a healthy and safe working environment, consider the following action tools:

- ✷ Obtain and review your company's health and safety policy and procedures and governing laws.
- ✷ Publicize the policy, procedures, and laws by clearly displaying them on bulletin boards and in employee manuals and publications, and by discussing them in meetings, employee orientations, and training sessions.
- ✷ Promote a healthy and safe workplace through your personal leadership, actions, and words.
- ✷ Seriously maintain all required health and safety reports and records.
- ✷ Become acquainted with your company's health and safety department, and seek advice and guidance from company medical and safety advisers.
- ✷ Encourage employee initiative and involvement on employee safety committees to help identify health and safety risks and hazards, and to improve workplace conditions.

37

Cultivating Entrepreneurial Spirit

Case Problem: "Clash of the Titans"

Last month, Ann, a systems analyst and independent contractor, made her long-planned career move to a full-time position as senior systems analyst with a major corporation.

She knew that as an employee within a corporate information management department she would no longer have to spend time on operating her business and, instead, could dedicate her energy to her systems work, her first love.

At one of her first department meetings, the group discussed a plan to hold an important three-day off-site training session. Leon, the director, mentioned the Royal Hanover Hotel located about thirty miles north of the office, as a possible location for the session.

While walking back to her cubicle following the meeting, Ann remembered attending a seminar at the Royal Hanover Hotel. "What an awful place!" she thought. She recalled a musty-smelling training room with very poor lighting and a noisy, defective heating system. She also recalled the indifferent attitude of the hotel staff and the difficulty in getting the beverages and snacks during the breaks.

Even if the Royal Hanover were a decent place, Ann wondered why Leon would have the entire department travel thirty miles from the office when the Viking Inn and Conference Center was only five minutes away. And what a great place, too! Ann had attended several meetings at the Viking Inn and knew it to be tops in conference center services.

The next day, Ann used her lunch time and drove over to the Viking Inn. She introduced herself to the sales manager and explained her interest in considering the Viking Inn for an upcoming meeting. After a brief discussion, the sales manager gave a quote for the upcoming session, which seemed very reasonable to Ann.

At the department meeting the following week, Ann mentioned her visit to the Viking Inn and Conference Center and her discussion with the sales manager. She passed around brochures of the facility, related her experiences while attending seminars there, and recommended the Viking Inn as a better alternative to the Royal Hanover Hotel.

Upon hearing her proposal, Ann's new colleagues gave her a round of applause, praising her efforts and results. Leon, however, just sat there with a forced smile on his face, saying, "Well, I'll look into this proposal and will take it into consideration."

At the following staff meeting, Leon informed the group they would have their off-site training at the Royal Hanover Hotel as he had originally intended. When questioned by Ann about the Viking Inn, Leon glared at Ann, exclaiming, "I've looked into the matter and have made up my mind. It will be the Royal Hanover. Next subject!"

Four weeks later, during the morning of the first day of training, Ann noticed that it was hard to hear the speaker or anyone else in the room. Apparently, a very loud air-conditioning unit in the ceiling was drowning out the voices as well as freezing the room.

During the lunch break, Ann walked over to the hotel's engineering office, explained the situation, and asked for immediate help. Within a half hour, a hotel engineer had repaired the ceiling unit.

Upon returning to the meeting after lunch, the employees noticed the more comfortable temperature and quieter ceiling unit and inquired about what had happened. "I saw that we were freezing and that our voices were being drowned out by the ceiling unit," Ann explained, "so I asked engineering to fix the problem."

Hearing about her results, the group thanked Ann and applauded her initiative. Leon, however, sat quietly, grinding his teeth and forcing a smile.

Upon the conclusion of the first day's work, Leon called Ann over to the side and admonished her.

"Ann, I don't know your game," he began. "All on your own, you tried to change our training facility, but you failed. And now you've gotten the hotel engineering department to mess around with our meeting room. Just remember this: I'm the boss, not you. If you're trying to show me up, forget it. You're not in your own business now. I run this department, not you. Do you understand?"

"But Leon, I was only trying to help," explained Ann, who was stunned by Leon's unexpected reaction and scolding. "And, in my business, I've always believed in the motto, 'The person who notices a problem, owns it.' All I did was take ownership for problems that needed handling!"

"In this department, if you notice a problem, tell me," said Leon, "and I'll decide what to do with it. Furthermore, until you arrived here, we had no problems. So from now on, pay attention to your own work and leave the business of running this department to me! Got it?"

Case Analysis

In this case, there is a clash of style between Ann, a former entrepreneur with an independent problem-solving spirit, and Leon, a boss obsessed with maintaining his authority and oblivious to opportunities for improvement.

As a successful small business owner, Ann had been totally responsible for her own success and totally in charge of her own business. She demanded the best of herself and delivered the best for her clients.

When obstacles blocked her path, she removed them. When opportunities for improvement became available, she took advantage of them. And in addition to providing the systems services to her clients, Ann successfully managed every aspect of her own business.

Leon, on the other hand, was totally content with his department as it was and saw Ann's unexpected improvement efforts as threats to his power and position. Rather than acknowledge Ann's initiatives—as the rest of the department had done—Leon angrily reacted, attempting to squelch any future initiatives.

It is clear from this case that Ann brought to her work great spirit, energy, and self-motivation. In addition, she appeared to care greatly about all she did and approached everything with pride and a strong sense of ownership. Such spirit can only enhance a department if it is properly acknowledged and channeled.

Unfortunately, because of Leon's selfish preoccupation with his own power and position, he bucked heads with Ann and missed a unique opportunity to discover and harness her invaluable entrepreneurial talent within the department.

Action Tools

To cultivate entrepreneurial spirit within your department, consider the following action tools:

- Value and welcome the independent spirit and business approach of entrepreneurial employees.
- Explain to them your team processes for operating within the department and interacting with other departments, and ask them to support these processes. At the same time, however, be receptive to recommendations for improvements that they may propose.
- Give them opportunities for assuming leadership roles on departmental projects and committees, and publicly recognize their passion, innovativeness and smart business savvy.
- See your department as a small independent business, operating within a large corporate setting and commissioned to deliver top-quality services to demanding internal or external customers. As such, explain to employees the possible risks of poor business performance: downsizing, merging with other corporate departments, or total elimination and replacement by outsourcing firms.
- Urge all employees to act as business owners and to dedicate themselves to protecting their department's business, and thereby their own positions, by driving up quality, productivity, and customer satisfaction while driving down costs and cycle times.

38

Creating a Caring Organization

Case Problem: "Sitting in Their Own Garbage"

Last year, Lester, vice president of sales and marketing at Goliath Steel, was recruited by Carl, chairman and founder of Magma Steel, to become Magma's new chief executive officer. Carl had built a $40 million-a-year business and was retiring after thirty years. His priority now, in addition to golf and fishing, was to see Magma become a $200 million business over the next five years; and he wanted a proven leader with marketing capability to lead his company into the future. During his first year at the helm, Lester focused on developing market image as a quality steel producer and getting greater global exposure.

Today, Lester is meeting in his office with two senior executives who are searching for a supplier to provide their company with quality steel for use in engine components for high speed trains. After reviewing technical requirements and brochures, as well as product samples manufactured with Magma steel, the executives examine the numbers. They appear enthusiastic and indicate their serious interest in an initial $5 million order.

Feeling great about his sales meeting, Lester invites the two executives to join him on a brief tour of Magma's steel-making facilities. As the men enter the main plant, one of the executives remarks to the other about the first thing he sees—a group of workers eating lunch.

"Pierre, look over there at those men," he says. "They're disgusting. They're sitting in their own garbage!"

Lester, startled by what he sees, tries to explain. "Gentlemen, you do realize it's lunch time now, and those workers are only eating their lunch."

"But, sir," exclaims Pierre, "they're sitting on garbage cans and throwing their garbage all over the work area. In fact, this whole plant is a pigsty!"

"Gentlemen," Lester replies, trying to salvage the situation, "the garbage on the plant floor has absolutely no effect on the quality of our products. And I can vouch for my workers. They do care and take their work very seriously."

Unconvinced by Lester's assurances, the executives turn to leave the plant when suddenly a pack of rats leaps out from behind the water cooler, scurrying across the men's path. Maurice, Pierre's associate, screams in fear as the lunch crowd on the plant floor points in amusement at the horrified visitors and fearless rodents.

Case Analysis

Lester knows little about his company's steel-making operations and even less about its management and workforce. In addition, he has spent little or no time in-house learning about his company's strengths and weaknesses.

While his efforts at creating a global market image and building new business relationships are laudable, his position as CEO demands that he act as a company-wide leader. This means drawing all his executives, functions, and resources together in an integrated effort to enhance total organizational quality, including product, process, leadership, and workforce.

The fact is that the management and workforce of Magma Steel display a total lack of concern for the company, their products, their jobs and, worst of all, themselves. While Lester claimed the people do care and take their work seriously, it is clear they do not.

It's unfortunate that Magma has lost a huge new account due to this situation. But now is the time to confront the problem and deal with it.

Action Tools

To create a caring organization, consider the following action tools:

✦ From the beginning, strive to staff your organization with individuals who are both technically qualified and caring people who approach their work with a sense of responsibility, dedication, and pride.

✦ Serve as a role model for your employees, teaching a caring attitude by your own example and actions.

✦ Institute a performance management process with all employees by setting clear expectations, providing regular feedback and coaching, and conducting performance development meetings.

✦ Practice "management by walking around" (MBWA) by getting out and personally visiting and observing all aspects of your operation.

✦ Any time you see examples of caring behavior, spotlight those achievements and recognize the individuals involved.

✦ If you observe examples of uncaring behavior among employees, such as neglected work areas, lack of initiative in taking care of problems, or inattentiveness to safety rules, speak to the individuals involved and help them develop immediate corrective action plans.

✦ Encourage regular problem-solving and continuous improvement among employees as means for enhancing their level of caring.

Section VI
Leadership

39

Leading People on a Day-to-Day Basis

Case Problem: "The Lost Leader"

"... and don't ever do that again," yelled Al, manager of product development, in the hall as Donald, a new product engineer, walked away in a hurry, humiliated and defeated.

Seeing the whole event right before her eyes, Rita felt embarrassed for Donald who she knew to be a hard-working and conscientious young engineer. "Al will get his one day," she thought as she recalled Al's critical and demeaning tactics with her and other members of the product development staff over the years.

Later that morning at the coffee machines, Rita met Jack, a fellow engineer who was sitting alone, looking troubled.

"Hey, Jack, why are you looking so down?" she asked.

"Don't ask," lamented Jack. "When will I learn that our trusting boss is only looking out for himself and the points he can score with management?"

"What did Al, our dear boss, do this time?" inquired Rita.

"Read this little blurb with Al's picture in the new idea section of our company newsletter," said Jack. "It says that Al devised the new RTC cost reduction procedure."

"Well, that's good, isn't it?" asked Rita.

"Sure," replied Jack. "The RTC procedure can save a heck of a lot of dollars for the company. There's just one thing wrong, though—the procedure was my idea. I was the one who worked it up and explained it to Al a month ago. He said at that time that it would never fly, that it was useless to this company. Well, can you imagine my shock in reading this article?"

Upon hearing Jack's story, Rita encouraged him to go directly to Al and confront him about the article.

"It wouldn't work," replied Jack. "The guy is a thief and will never admit the idea was mine. Furthermore, I never wrote it up and have no evidence to prove it."

Rita agreed, knowing full well Al's approach: to take all the credit when things went well but give all the blame when things went wrong.

At that moment, Al, the manager, entered the coffee room with a sneer on his face.

"Ah ha, so here you are, Rita, goofing off when you should be at your desk working up that report you owe me this afternoon,"

Turning to her boss with a triumphant look on her face, Rita said that the report was already completed and would be delivered to his office by the end of the day.

"I hope it takes into consideration our new personnel policy," commented Al, as he walked out of the coffee room with a sarcastic smile on his face.

"I hate those sarcastic sparring games of his," thought Rita. "He never told me anything about a new personnel policy. What's he trying to pull, anyway?

"This is the third time this month that he has failed to inform me of important company policy changes that affect my work. Well, now he can live with the report as it is. I'm not revising it because of his lack of communication."

In the cafeteria, Al joined his friend Tom, the production superintendent, for lunch. "So, Al, how are your engineers shaping up these days?" inquired Tom. "What can you expect from a bunch of lazy incompetents?" complained Al. "I've had nothing but trouble with those people since I started this job five years ago. You've got to stay on top of them every minute, or they'll goof off or try to get away with something."

As Al was complaining, one of Tom's people—Sue, the production planner—courteously interrupted, asking Tom for a quick explanation of a new job to be run. Tom excused himself for a minute, explaining the job to Sue right there at the table.

"There, Sue, does that make sense to you?" asked Tom.

"You bet," replied Sue. "I really appreciate your helpfulness, Tom." Then, turning to Al with pride, Sue commented, "I've got just about the best boss anyone could ever want. Tom is always there to support and encourage each one of us."

"Well, Al, I guess I'm more fortunate with my staff than you are," said Tom as Sue walked away. "I try to give my people as much freedom as possible to perform and try to encourage them to take initiative. With me it works. I'm real proud of them."

Al's only reaction was an insincere smile and a half-hearted acknowledgment of Tom's comments.

Case Analysis

A manager has the responsibility for leading the staff on a day-to-day basis. This regular effort requires a positive attitude toward people and a clear understanding of how to maintain harmonious relations and encourage full participation within a team effort.

In the case above, however, a manager's every encounter with his staff is filled with friction, sarcasm, put-downs, distrust, threats and general bad feelings. Even in Al's conversations with employees outside of product development, he conveys a low regard for his people and reveals an inability to lead in a positive and productive manner.

Action Tools

To build an effective leadership style, consider the following action tools:

- ✳ Demonstrate genuine respect for your employees and their talent, and give sincere praise for their work.
- ✳ Give as much freedom in performing jobs as the staff can handle in order to convey trust in their ability and encourage their professional development.
- ✳ Serve as the company information link, conveying current and needed information to the staff to satisfy both job and personal needs.
- ✳ Provide honest and helpful feedback to employees on

job performance, and be ready to coach them for immediate work improvement.

★ When talking with individuals both within and outside
the department, convey pride in your people and your
group's accomplishments.

40

Building Management Influence

Case Problem: "The Powerless Manager"

Following the weekly management staff meeting, Mike, the general manager, asks Carl, the plant controller, to stay behind for a private discussion. Mike is upset by Carl's behavior in the meeting and needs to clear the air on other matters as well.

"Mike, I wonder if you are properly qualified to maintain the full authority of the plant controller's position at this time. I'm just not sure whether I can trust you to lead your people by example as a member of our management team."

"How can you say that?" asks Carl. "You can count on me to get things done in accounting and to help out on any company business of importance."

"That's just it," explains Mike. "I can think of several instances in which you failed to score any points around here. And, in each case, your professional image and influence have been seriously hurt.

"First, you had no right to attack Lenny personally and humiliate the other managers on the manufacturing planning committee during our meeting. Those managers spent months working together to develop a critical new process for our plant. You, on the other hand, didn't lift a finger to help them in spite of being asked to on several occasions. There's no question in my mind that your peer relations are at an all-time low.

"Then, there was the time I needed the data on our new office equipment for my report to corporate staff. You failed to get it to me, and I had to fake it, looking like a real fool that day.

"And a month ago, I gave you an opportunity to serve on an important corporate committee dealing with compensation. You could have scored some winning points for the plant, accounting and yourself. But, no, you were too busy. Now that would have been great. You have a special expertise in salary administration matters that you developed at Cole & Company.

"And what about the time the new president flew over from Texas to inspect our facility in March? You came to work that day looking like a mess. I was embarrassed, and there were many comments, too.

"Finally, it's hard to trust and support someone who continues to go over my head to my boss, the vice president of operations, to question and argue my every decision. No, Carl, something has to change and soon. And until it does, you've got no clout with me."

"I'll show you, Mike," said Carl. "My accounting staff holds me in high esteem. They respect me, I just know it."

Walking quickly to the office of one of his accounting supervisors, Carl quickly sat down.

"Roger, I'm having a bad day," he sighed. "Tell me the truth. You and the staff really respect me, don't you? And aren't you putting your best foot forward to work with me?"

"I can only speak for myself and tell you what I know," declared Roger. "But the fact is I'm afraid to give my opinion. You know, you may not like what I have to say. But if you allow me to have David and Nancy join us, I'd feel better leveling with you. And it's off the record, too, right?"

"If that's what it takes, O.K.," agreed the controller.

After getting David and Nancy, two others from accounting, into his office, Roger began to open up.

"Respect, loyalty, cooperation. Man, you've gotta be kidding. When you started here, coming from another company in North Carolina, you didn't even care that I was the one up for the position of controller. Not one word from you about being sorry that you stole my job."

"I didn't realize you felt that way, Roger," explained Carl, regretfully. "I really should have spoken with you sooner about your feelings."

"And what about me and the rest of the staff?" interrupted David. "You've never taken the time with any of us to find out who we are and what makes us tick. It's always David do this, David do that. Who cares about what I'd prefer to do or what types of assignments turn people on or off?"

"And when we have a problem," added Nancy, "we get grief, not help. You expect respect and loyalty with that kind of treatment?"

As Carl listened, he started feeling sick but kept quiet.

"And let's not forget all the extra work we've done," Nancy continued. "Instead of hearing some sincere thanks or praise from our 'caring' boss, we end up feeling used and degraded for having tried."

"I think what we're all saying," said Roger, "is that a boss who fails to reward employees, fails to treat them fairly, and, most of all, fails to recognize that they are human beings can never win the trust, respect, or loyalty of these employees."

Stunned by this discussion, as well as the earlier management session and conversation, Carl was speechless. It was now painfully clear to him that he wielded no influence with anyone in the company.

Case Analysis

Carl, a plant controller, alienated rather than cultivated important people—people who could have supported his efforts within the company. Carl failed to gain the trust and respect of peers, executives, and employees alike. Consequently, their cooperation and loyalty to him were not offered.

For all intents and purposes, Carl was a controller without personal power or influence to get results with and through people. His manager could not trust him and would not back him. In addition, his manager would not recommend him for other higher-level tasks, rewards, or promotions.

His peers, who were in a position to share company resources, helpful information, and friendship, were alienated by Carl's standoffish nonteamplayer attitude. Instead of becoming influential among his fellow managers and winning needed cooperation for accounting, Carl had isolated the department, as he had isolated himself from the management team.

Carl desperately seeks self-assurance in his last refuge—the accounting staff—where respect and support for him as controller may still exist. But here, too, he finds a lack of trust and even deep-seated hostility.

While Carl may still possess official power to require staff work, a greater power—the willing and enthusiastic cooperation of others—is clearly not there. This greater power is created when a manager is accepted as a sincere and caring human being, ready to express appreciation; as a person of knowledge, expertise, and skill, ready to help; as a person admired and respected by associates and superiors; and as a well-connected leader, ready to represent the department within the organization and keep his or her staff abreast of important company matters.

Action Tools

A manager's personal power to influence the feelings, thoughts, or actions of others is essential for the successful accomplishment of departmental goals. The following actions are recommended for building a solid sphere of influence to achieve departmental objectives and advance your management career:

* Recognize that power is conveyed to the manager, not only in the form of formal authority by the organization, but also by peers and employees as they willingly extend themselves in cooperation to assist and support the manager.
* Exercise your present formal authority to the limit with skill and proficiency. Then, seek to enhance your authority, having earned the trust and respect of management.
* Build relationships with all individuals and become recognized as their problem solver, not their problem creator.
* Seek opportunities to share your knowledge, expertise, and skills. In so doing, you will be held in high esteem by others who will seek opportunities to reciprocate your thoughtfulness.
* See yourself as a need satisfier first, carefully assessing the other's needs, then helping to satisfy them. Whatever the need—information, recognition, counseling, or coaching—such a commitment to others' needs is generally responded to by the enhanced cooperation and dedication of others.

✳ Associate with peers as well as with other executives inside your organization to build a mutual help network as well as enhance your professional image.

✳ Be sure to present a positive, uplifting, and professional image through your appearance, behavior, and communications. Attention to your personal image always pays off in greater respect, admiration, and enhanced influence.

41

Promoting From Within

Case Problem: "Movin' On Up"

"I'm sick and tired of the way I'm being treated around here," complained Greg, the new information systems manager, to Roberta, a friend from the sales department. "I just don't understand it. I get no respect. Don't they realize I'm the manager now? They just don't take me seriously."

"That's strange," replied Roberta. "I would think if you did come up from the ranks, as you have, people would really respect you and work with you."

"I thought so, too," continued Greg, "but something has definitely gone wrong. They don't seem to accept my leadership, but instead still regard me as a fellow systems analyst. They put off projects that I give them, even though these projects have specific deadlines. And they think nothing of telling me they'll get to it when they can. I'm beginning to feel like the fool around here.

"And you know what, Roberta? One of my so-called friends said that now with me at the helm, he could start relaxing. He said that to a couple of other people in the department. I heard it with my own ears."

Case Analysis

Management positions can be filled by candidates from outside or through internal promotions from within a company. While outside hires offer a company important benefits, internal promotions have many important advantages as well. These include hiring a manager with technical expertise in the group's work, an intimate knowledge of the special needs of the department, a thorough acquaintance with company policies and procedures, and a proven track record of company loyalty.

Along with the advantages of internal promotions, however, come drawbacks. In the case above, Greg, the new information systems manager, is experiencing these problems.

Since his recent promotion from the ranks of systems analysts, Greg feels frustrated and angry by his inability to gain the cooperation of his former peers in his new management role. He experiences attempts by former coworkers to downplay or discount his new management responsibilities and authority. Some even attempt to exploit the new manager in the name of friendship.

Action Tools

To ensure a successful internal management promotion, consider the following action tools:

* During a staff meeting of the entire department, senior management should formally and publicly introduce a newly promoted manager as the official department head with full authority and responsibility for departmental operations.
* Senior management should make it clear to all employees at that time that the new manager will require full and complete cooperation.
* The new manager should use this important meeting to spell out his/her expectations for the new working relationships in the department and to solicit everyone's cooperation in making the new relationships work.
* Immediately following this meeting, the new manager should set up a one-on-one meeting with each employee to solicit individual ideas and personal cooperation.

42

Leading by Example

Case Problem: "The Wrong Example"

"Al, I'm upset with a few things you've been doing around here," complained Rick, the purchasing manager, to a buyer.

"What are you talking about, Rick? I've been doing my job—I see no problems," replied Al, defensively.

"Well, if you're so innocent, what do you call a four-cocktail lunch?" inquired Rick. "Since you've come on board, you've been taking two hours for lunch every day in addition to hour-long breaks in the morning and afternoon. Don't you think I've been aware of that?"

"But I'm getting my work done," reacted Al. "And I never really thought those lunch and coffee break rules applied around here, anyway."

"You've gotta be kidding," responded Rick. "What makes you so unique? Rules are rules and must be followed."

"Honestly, Rick, I knew the rule but never really thought you were serious about it," argued Al. "After all, whenever I'm relaxing, socializing, or eating, you're usually around, too. I've only followed your lead."

While Al and Rick were having this discussion, Betty, another buyer in the department, was showing Gary, a colleague, a report she had submitted to Rick, her manager.

"You know, Gary, the boss just rejected this report, complaining it was too formal with too much supporting data. In addition, he put down my writing style. Can you believe that? I was an English minor in college. The guy is a near illiterate himself. Where does he come off judging my report?"

"It's true!" exclaimed Gary. "He's in no position to criticize anybody else's writing, especially yours. You write beautifully. Here, look at these memos he puts together. They're laughable. If you want my opinion, Betty, I wouldn't put so much time into your reports. Maybe he's angry and jealous because he thinks you're showing him up."

As the two colleagues spoke, Rick walked into their room to remind them of an 11 AM meeting.

"It's 11:10 already, and you people are ten minutes late for my meeting. I know you don't appreciate your own schedules, but why can't you appreciate mine?"

Gary and Betty put their papers together quickly and walked to Rick's office.

"The guy is unreal," Gary commented. "He's never on time for his own staff meetings and now, the one time that he is, he expects us to be there waiting for him."

Once the meeting began, it progressed very slowly, as Rick moved through the agenda at a snail's pace, in boring detail. While Rick was reading a new policy statement from upstairs, Betty bent over to Gary and whispered sarcastically.

"The power and enthusiasm of this guy are simply overwhelming," she said. "What do you think?"

"It's true," agreed Gary, jokingly. "I really get an uplift and a desire to conquer the world when listening to that exciting voice."

When Rick finished reading the statements, he looked up at the group only to see boredom and apathy on the faces of his staff.

"Why me?" thought Rick. "Why am I blessed with a bunch of dull-witted employees?"

Case Analysis

Here, a department manager's behavior appears to adversely affect each member of the staff. Through his own behavior, Rick sets the standards and the tone for inferior performance, abuse of rules, and general apathy.

In the case of Al, who regularly takes extra long lunch and coffee breaks, the manager condones such indifference to rules through his own example.

Betty, a conscientious buyer trying to prepare the best possible project report, finds it difficult to accept the criticism of her manager, who is considered illiterate by his staff. What's worse, Betty may now intentionally lower her higher standards to avoid "showing up" her boss.

Rick's criticism of Gary and Betty's tardiness seems inconsistent with always showing up late himself for meetings. It is unfair and inconsiderate for Rick to pass such a judgment on his staff since his own past actions have directly encouraged staff tardiness.

At the meeting, there is apathy and indifference on the part of the staff. Of course, this is clearly a reaction to Rick's lack of enthusiasm and uninspired leadership.

Action Tools

Leading by example—sometimes known as role modeling—is a powerful management tool that the manager can utilize to inspire enthusiasm in raising employee performance. As the team leader, the manager possesses the power and status to directly influence—by his or her own behavior—the standards, goals, and values of the staff. In communicating rules, regulations, and standards of performance, the manager has the opportunity to serve as a model by personally following these guidelines and thereby providing actual proof of their importance.

The manager should set a personal example of high standards in the following critical areas of behavior to motivate staff and achieve optimal departmental results:

* Convey enthusiasm and a positive attitude when dealing with the staff.
* Personally conform with all rules and regulations that apply to the staff.
* Demonstrate high energy, initiative, and optimism in approaching work, and search for new and creative solutions to departmental problems.
* Communicate a genuine desire to understand your employees' needs and frustrations and to assist in improving their professional performance and resolving their individual problems. They, in turn, will reciprocate with the same dedication and loyalty.
* Exhibit strength, honesty, and tact in confronting individuals with problems and reaching satisfactory solutions.

✳ Take extra care to communicate face to face and in writing with skill, clarity, conviction, and enthusiasm.

✳ Utilize effectively all your available resources to support each staff member in doing the best possible work.

✳ Encourage employee participation in problem-solving and decision-making.

✳ Continuously refine old skills and develop new skills that will enable you to better achieve your management objectives and personal career goals.

✳ Foster teamwork and cooperation by demonstrating your own team skills in all your encounters with staff, colleagues, and management.

43

Using the Appropriate Leadership Style

Case Problem: "The Team Breaker"

Arnold, the manager of industrial engineering, has been with his new company for approximately four weeks. Before coming on board, he had worked for a company with serious staffing and financial problems and concluded from that experience that an iron hand was needed to get results from staff.

As a result of his past experience, he has become a caustic manager, with very little concern for the individual needs or problems of his staff members. At his new company, his behavior over the past month has already prompted a few of his people to start sending out resumes.

At a recent staff meeting, Arnold harshly criticized the work of one of the senior methods analysts.

"Sam, you don't have all your facts together," he said. "This is a real sloppy job from what I can see. And the rest of you people, you're going to require some tight guidelines, or all the work you do will end up looking like this garbage Sam has just presented."

Sam sank back in his chair, completely embarrassed by his new boss's comments on his project that was still in its developmental stage.

Later that afternoon over coffee, a couple of staff members discussed the deteriorating condition of their department as a result of their new manager's heavy-handed style.

"You saw the way he treated Sam in the meeting," griped Carl. "Sam is a pro. Arnold had no right to do that. Furthermore, it's insulting the way he glares at people and points his finger right into their eyes.

"It's crazy. We used to have a solid team here. Now, this new guy comes in and throws his weight around, acting like a real heavy!"

"I know," commiserated Joan. "Why, just the other day, I heard him reprimand Alice for making a suggestion. He said he's the boss, and if he ever wants any advice, he certainly wouldn't turn to a subordinate for it. You know, Carl, we're not a group of school kids. We're a department of professionals."

"I agree," responded Carl. "I give the guy about three months before the resignations start coming in. I can't take him myself. In fact, after coffee, I'm going to update my own resume."

Case Analysis

Conflicts such as these are certain to occur under a manager with an inappropriate, heavy-handed leadership style. Such a style can seriously hurt the morale and effectiveness of a team, resulting in discouraged employees and heavy turnover.

The new manager has been treating his staff as though they are no different from the "problem" employees he encountered in his former position. But in reality, Arnold's new department is staffed by team players who are highly motivated, very knowledgeable professionals. And the members of this team have clearly been thrown by their new manager's readiness to abuse them and discount their efforts in public.

Action Tools

A manager should follow these guidelines for appropriate leadership of a department:

* Upon assuming the position of manager, get to know the members of your staff, their individual strengths and weaknesses, problems, and needs.
* Do not allow any negative situations from previous management positions influence your attitude or behavior toward your new staff. Such unfair judgments and treatment of new staff will surely cause disintegration of a fine team.

✦ Provide closer supervision with more feedback and coaching to employees who need to improve their performance.

✦ Give greater freedom and independence to employees who operate in a highly professional manner.

✦ Communicate your vision and expectations for effective teamwork, encouraging high employee involvement and participation in important department activities.

✦ Practice common courtesy and good human relations at all times, regardless of whether you've having a good or bad day.

44

Empowering Your Employees

Case Problem: "The Micromanager"

Going through her mail, Lilian, a manager with the information management department, came across a letter marked urgent and personal from Donald, one of her employees. Lilian quickly opened the letter and read it with disbelief:

Dear Lilian:

    Congratulations! You have successfully stifled my initiative in this job and nearly destroyed my self-esteem and crushed my spirit.

    I offered you my best, which you have consistently rejected. Therefore, I now offer you the only thing I have left: my resignation!

    One year ago, I joined the company with great hope and a desire to contribute my skill and talent and to continue my career development. During my first few weeks on the job, I welcomed your daily coaching, your many suggestions, and your frequent advice on how to perform the details of my work.

    As I became familiar with the company's systems and procedures, I thanked you for your initial help and asked for greater freedom and authority. Instead, you "pulled in the reins," monitoring my every move, questioning me at every turn, and frequently changing or completely overruling my day-to-day job decisions.

    Lilian, I am a professional with twelve years of successful

experience. I have worked hard to earn my stripes. But during this year, you have treated me with insensitivity and lack of respect as if I were a junior trainee.

Frustrated by your continuous and unceasing scrutiny of my work, I endured your ongoing interference and put-downs. But the straw that broke the camel's back was my recent review in which you so unfairly condemned my initiative and criticized me for my unwillingness to take direction and my refusal to accept your criticism.

Lilian, I now leave this company with one final thought: "Get A Life!" I'm finally taking mine back!

Sincerely,

Donald

cc: V.P. Information Management
    Director of Human Resources

P.S. You may as well know. I have the courage to resign "*from this job.*" Look around. You have caused everyone else in the department to resign "*on* the job."

Case Analysis

Lilian is a classic example of a micromanager: a manager who spends excessive time and energy closely monitoring and over-controlling the details of employee work.

As a micromanager, Lilian was inappropriately and overly concerned with the smallest and pettiest details of day-to-day work.

Donald, an experienced, confident, and competent professional welcomed Lilian's initial behavior as helpful coaching and caring orientation. Soon, however, he came to realize that Lilian's apparent concern and great attentiveness to the details of his work were, in fact, uncalled for and stifling.

Lilian's persistence in hovering over and constantly correcting Donald's every move was perceived as intrusiveness, interference, and condescension, which led to feelings of discouragement, frustration, and anger. The more freedom, authority, and independence Donald sought, the more controlling Lilian became.

Donald's ultimate act was to resign "from the job." By doing so, Donald may have saved himself. However, as he points out in his letter's "P. S.," the rest of the staff has effectively resigned "on the job."

Micromanagement is not a productive management style. Rather, it is a dysfunctional form of management that restricts, hampers, frustrates, and unempowers employees who would otherwise assume greater ownership of their own work.

Unfortunately, too many managers practice micromanagement, overcontrolling their employees and discouraging employee initiative, ownership, and professional growth and development. Some of the common reasons include:

- Lack of trust in employees who may "mess things up"
- Belief that "I can do the work better and faster myself"
- Belief that it will take too long to train others
- Fear of losing personal recognition and prestige for work well done
- Fear of losing authority
- Failure to understand and practice the legitimate higher-level responsibilities of management

Action Tools

Great management is about helping others to succeed and achieve great results by helping them develop knowledge and skills and by encouraging initiative, motivation, creativity, risk-taking, and pride of personal job ownership.

Avoid, at all costs, any tendency to micromanage employees. Micromanagement unempowers employees, inhibits personal development, stifles healthy decision-making and risk-taking, and restricts team productivity. By constantly scrutinizing every minor detail of employee work, micromanagers are major sources of low employee morale.

To overcome the tendency to micromanage, consider implementing the following important action tools:

* Keep the right focus. When delegating an assignment, focus your attention on what you expect and when you expect it. On the other hand, encourage employees to focus their attention on the best ways of executing their assignments and solving the day-to-day problems of the job.

* Train and trust your employees. Make certain they have the required skills and knowledge, either through prior experience, formal training, or on-the-job coaching. Then, demonstrate your trust by giving them the freedom and space to "test their own wings and take to flight." The results may be spectacular.

* Assume greater responsibility for leading your team within the larger organization. By doing so, you will be perfecting your expertise of management while your employees will achieve greater proficiency and efficiency in handling their own rightful responsibilities.

* Commit yourself, your time, and your energy to encouraging, motivating, and recognizing employee initiative and achievements.

* Delegate maximum authority to employees so they can personally control their own work and make necessary day-to-day decisions within prescribed boundaries. By doing so, you will gain employee respect, extend your sphere of authority, and save yourself valuable time.

45

Managing Diversity

Case Problem: "Diversity Adversity"

Two months ago, fifty new employees from different countries arrived at the corporate headquarters of a large American diversified financial services company. This company had plans to develop new markets and operations in various Eastern European and Asian countries and sought to develop local talent to help staff these new international sites. The fifty new employees would work in the United States for up to sixteen months to learn the business and then transfer their knowledge back to their countries' new facilities.

Today, Lane, president of the company, held an executive meeting and discussed the situation of the fifty international employees.

"Ladies and gentlemen," he began. "As you know, each of you has been assigned a number of new employees representing a variety of countries that we have targeted for business development. Unfortunately, our efforts in this area have not been as effective as I had hoped. Marcel, our vice president of human resources, requested anonymous feedback from these employees last week and would now like to share the group's comments with you."

"I will quote representative comments from the group," Marcel began, "which will give you a strong sense of their initial experiences and impressions of our company."

Then, Marcel read the following anonymous, candid comments from various new employees:

"I felt slighted at my first staff meeting when my manager failed to mention my name or introduce me to my new colleagues."
"My English is very poor. Everyone speaks very quickly using all

those American idioms and company expressions so that I understand very little."

"When I started, I was given a job to do. But nobody took the time to review the procedures or relationships within the department and company."

"My manager became very upset when I did not submit a report that I promised to get to her. I would have gotten it to her sometime next week. I don't understand. I can be trusted to do what I say."

"In my department, there are groups of friends that speak the same language and have lunch together each day. I have joined the Spanish-speaking people, but they speak only Spanish. I've also joined the Nigerians, but I don't understand their language either. Even when I join the people who speak English, I'm not very good at English. It's as if I'm not even there. I feel so excluded."

"My boss humiliated me at a department meeting by telling me in front of my peers that I was stupid and that I showed no ability in my field. I know he was angry because I don't participate very much and tend to go along with the opinions of others."

"I feel like quitting and going back to my country. Two weeks ago, while working on a project in my cubicle, I overheard other workers saying that the new international employees will lower our standards. I am deeply hurt."

Case Analysis

In this case, we see a large company with a vital new global development strategy having difficulty integrating its new diverse international workforce.

From the feedback given by the new workers, it appears that the company will need to communicate a much stronger and clearer message to all employees about the importance of its new global plans and the critical value of utilizing local talent within its targeted Eastern European and Asian markets.

The company will also have to deal with a serious lack of good manners in welcoming new people on board. And, of particular importance, it will need to address a lack of awareness, appreciation, and respect for people from other cultures and nations, and for people who speak other languages.

Finally, the company will need to communicate its vision and commitment for the fullest development and utilization of each and every employee. Moreover, it will need to take immediate action for building trust, effective communication, and positive working relationships among its diverse workforce.

Action Tools

To effectively manage a diverse workforce, consider the following action tools:

* Communicate your commitment to managing a diverse workforce. The business marketplace and applicant pools are becoming increasingly more diverse, and workforce diversity is an irrefutable fact.
* Ensure that employees, regardless of their individual differences such as race, national origin, age, or disability, are fully developed and truly capable of performing quality work.
* When introducing new individuals to work groups, make sure to acknowledge their accomplishments and value their presence as part of the teams. Such initial positive support from the leader can help speed up group acceptance of new individuals, help them overcome initial shyness, and encourage more rapid involvement and participation.
* Develop an appreciation for multicultural and multinational differences. Learning how people may differ in such areas as their orientation to time, power, formality, risk, relationships, and communication can help you become a more understanding, adaptable, flexible, and effective leader.
* If someone's cultural orientation is in conflict with your company's culture, values, or rules, talk to the individual and clarify your organization's needs and requirements clearly and tactfully. You may want to consult with your manager, diversity specialist, or human resources representative for helpful advice.

✦ When an American company brings on board individuals who speak little or no English, get them trained in the English language quickly. Do not skip or stretch out this key learning activity.

✦ Take the opportunity to learn some key phrases of your new employee's native language. Such thoughtfulness will help in building mutual respect.

Section VII

Handling Problems
and Resolving
Conflicts

46

Resolving Problems and Conflicts Quickly and Honestly

Case Problem: "The Silent Treatment"

At 8 AM on St. Valentine's Day, Frank, the general accounting manager, was filling out a Valentine's card to give Barb, a long-term senior accountant in his department.

"Nothing like a Valentine's card to make everything all right," he thought. "I guess she's learned her lesson by now. After all, four weeks of the silent treatment should cure anybody, even a tough cookie like Barb."

Frank had been giving Barb the silent treatment for a month. He was mad at her for something that he couldn't even remember. Later that morning, while looking up at the wall clock, Frank noticed that it was 10:30.

"Where's Barb?" he wondered. "She's two hours late for work. That's not like her."

At that moment a sharp ringing of the phone broke the silence. It was Larry, Barb's husband. As Larry spoke, Frank sat down, overcome by a sinking feeling.

Larry broke the news that Barb had decided to quit because there had been a complete and irrevocable breakdown in her working relationship with Frank. She was so angry at Frank's behavior, Larry explained, that she didn't even want to speak to him.

Feeling numb, Frank could only think of how he'd behaved during that month. He then listened to Larry tell him how, over the years, Barb had loved working for Frank in the accounting department, but this was no longer the case.

Case Analysis

What Frank did to Barb, a loyal long-term employee, was unprofessional, inexcusable, and stupid. Torturing employees by purposefully not communicating for lengthy periods to make a point or teach a lesson is totally unacceptable and highly aggressive behavior.

Frank should not have been surprised when learning of Barb's resignation. No matter what Barb may have said or done, nothing justifies such a hostile and immature management response.

Action Tools

Consider the following action tools when resolving conflicts and problems:

- ✦ Never use underhanded tactics such as the silent treatment or guilt trip to hurt an employee or force an employee's hand. Such devious approaches only destroy relationships by undercutting trust and honesty.
- ✦ When a conflict does arise between you and a member of the staff, move quickly to resolve the problem, make amends, and recement the relationship.
- ✦ Talk directly to the person with whom you're having a conflict. By being straightforward and tactfully placing your cards on the table, it is likely that the issue at hand can be quickly resolved.

47

Acting Assertively With Courage and Confidence

Case Problem: "The Fearful Manager"

While sunning himself on the beach in Acapulco, Mexico, George, a manager for Carlyle Machinery, confided in his wife, Sonia:

"I wish everything were this beautiful and relaxing. But, Sonia, since becoming director of maintenance last year, every waking hour has been filled with stress. I am afraid of everything and everybody. I am afraid to make a mistake or step on the wrong toe. You know, this job is a step up and means an awful lot."

Listening to her husband, Sonia remembered how hard George had worked to get this position. He had always been a fighter; so how could he say such things now?

"Sam, one of my supervisors, does whatever he wants," George continued. "The other day, I asked him to handle an important assignment, but he refused, saying he had other things to do. I was afraid to object. He's been there seven years longer than I. And I think he's got some high-level connections.

"And, I know that all my people, as well as my secretary, Mary, have no respect for me. Last month, one of our meetings turned into a gripe session about all the things we need—and don't have—in our department, while all the other areas have all the resources they need. I'll admit that I'm afraid to make waves upstairs and ask for the things we need to do good work in maintenance."

As George was speaking, Sonia thought, "How can George live with such fears at work when he had always seemed so confident?"

Case Analysis

In this case, George, a conscientious, career-oriented manager, has fallen victim to his own fears. Although he has assertively displayed strength, know-how, and courage and had achieved success in his past, his new management situation had evoked powerful new fears that dominate his thoughts and impede his effectiveness.

When great changes occur in areas of life such as health, relationships, finances, and careers, our minds are often flooded with fears that sometimes are genuine concerns but more often are worries that never come to pass. Whether justifiable concerns or imagined worries, fears stop us from doing the things we want and limit our potential.

For George, as for anyone experiencing great life changes, it is extremely important to understand how fears can emotionally block our desires and thwart our efforts. George can regain his career momentum, but only if he deals effectively with the fears that have imprisoned him.

Action Tools

To help you deal assertively with fears that sap our energy and inhibit our effectiveness, consider the following action tools:

* Ask an individual you trust to help you understand and talk through fears that may be blocking your effectiveness.
* Explain that you are having difficulty in doing the things you need to do for fear that something negative will happen if you try.
* Write down the things you want to do and the fears that are blocking you, as in the following examples:

> "If I criticize Bob for his lateness, I am afraid that he will get angry and storm out of the room."
> "If I speak up at the team meeting, I am afraid that my associates won't take me seriously."

✳ Once your fears are listed clearly on paper, ask your friend to encourage you to talk about each of them and to challenge you to provide proof and evidence to support your negative beliefs. As you talk about your desires and their associated fears, it will become clear that many of your worries and concerns either have no basis in fact or are not as terrible as you may be imagining.

✳ Remember, assertive people can achieve their objectives because of self-confidence and the ability to understand, confront, and work through the fears that plague us all.

48

Counseling Employees With Work Performance Problems

Case Problem: "The Disheartened Achiever"

"I didn't get the promotion?" asked Tom, head teller at the Commerce Branch of First City Bank. "What do you mean? I'm the best qualified for the night manager's job. You know I know my stuff, You've never had any problems or complaints about me and my work."

"Look, Tom," replied Larry, the branch manager, "just last week I was informed that you stood back while a couple of your tellers were abusive to bank customers. Your failure to step in and handle that situation is unacceptable to me. Also, I'm aware of other problems you've been having in your current job. But that's beside the point. . . . My mind is made up."

Tom, totally disheartened at the end of this conversation, sank into a slump. Over the next three months, Tom felt his energy slipping away. He couldn't even do basic management tasks such as giving helpful feedback to employees regarding their job performance.

Over coffee one afternoon, Grace, a manager from the check processing department, talked with Tom.

"I know you're disappointed about being turned down for the job," she said. "I guess the timing wasn't just right. But both of us know you've got the drive and ability. It will happen. Be patient. You've been in a terrible slump ever since you didn't get that promotion."

Case Analysis

In this situation, Tom, a career-oriented individual striving to move ahead in his bank, became disheartened when he didn't reach his mark as expected. In such frustrating situations, it is vital for a manager to provide the career-minded employee with supportive counseling and realistic performance improvement planning.

In this case, Larry, the branch manager, merely conveyed his negative decision to Tom, offering no personal support or constructive action plans for future success. Fortunately for Tom, though, a caring manager from another department offered him the emotional support and helpful advice he needed.

Action Tools

When dealing with a disheartened employee, consider the following action tools:

* Be aware of employee frustrations and disappointments that can be caused by job or career setbacks.
* Realize that disheartened employees are emotional drains on themselves as well as the entire team.
* Take the initiative and time to counsel your disheartened employees.
* Be empathetic and encourage disheartened employees to talk about their hopes and frustrations.
* Help them to identify the causes of their job or career setbacks.
* Work with them in developing performance improvement plans to help them get back on track.

49

Supporting Employee Achievements to Management

Case Problem: "The Defense"

"Look, I think he deserves the full eight percent increase," argued Alice to her manager. "I'm going to fight for him and see that he gets it. After all, he is my most loyal, hard-working employee. I can always depend on him, no matter what."

Alice had worked in the public relations department for four years and just eight months ago had assumed the responsibilities of corporate communications manager. She was now taking a firm position with Harry, the director of public relations, and defending a raise for Jeff, a writer/editor on the company newsletter for about seven years.

Since working with Alice, Jeff had started to show definite signs of improvement in his performance. He was still the faithful employee he'd always been, but surprisingly, he now started to demonstrate a lot of initiative in his job and was beginning to generate top results and many new excellent ideas.

In the past, Jeff worked under Harry's direct supervision, and their personality clashes were well known throughout the company.

"Harry, he's not the same guy that worked for you," Alice said, continuing the conversation. "I only ask that you let me judge his performance based on my own observations, not on your feelings, biases, or past personality differences.

"We are not talking about a lot of money here. It boils down to only a few dollars a week, and we can handle it. I believe that giving Jeff the performance review and merit pay he deserves will spur him on to do the best he can.

"And, Harry, I think if Jeff knew that management was willing to stand up for his increase, he'd continue doing the super job he's been doing since he started working with me eight months ago. He goes far beyond the call of duty, and you know that."

"Well," reacted Harry, "I remember when Jeff worked directly for me. He was just looking for a safe and secure job. He had no ambition. He was never my type of man."

"With all due respect to you," responded Alice, "all of that is in the past. Jeff has performed successfully for me, and we owe it to him to award him the full eight percent that he has earned. Anything less will undermine my position as corporate communications manager in this department."

Case Analysis

In this case, Alice successfully motivated Jeff and was able to get positive results from him. Now, Jeff is expecting an equitable performance review and merit increase. It is important that Alice convinces Harry to support her judgment and not allow past relationships and biases to destroy the new momentum developed over the past eight months.

If Harry truly wants Alice to strengthen her leadership role as a manager, he should grant her request for the eight percent increase.

Action Tools

In supporting employee achievements to management, consider the following action tools:

* ✴ Equitably administer your merit pay program, which can provide important incentives to improve performance.
* ✴ Base your performance reviews and merit decisions on actual job accomplishments.
* ✴ Stand up for your employees' achievements by getting "earned" merit dollars approved by management.

50

Giving Constructive Criticism Properly

Case Problem: "The Heavy-Handed Approach"

"I've had it with this job and your big mouth," said Mike, storming out of the building.

He had just been reprimanded in public for the last time by Bob, the production manager, who had a terrible habit of viciously attacking people on the production floor. He had done this to Mike one time too many.

Mike, was a promising employee. In fact, he was spotted by the big brass as true management material. He was a top equipment operator, but when it came to dealing with Bob, he became flustered.

Bob was around from the start of the company. He always used a heavy-handed approach to get his way around the department. He used his volume to intimidate and embarrass his employees. After eight months of this, Mike had reached his saturation point.

As Mike walked out, Bob smirked to himself, "Some management material. Ha!"

Case Analysis

In this case, the manager needlessly insulted and alienated Mike, a top operator. The manager's pattern of giving destructive criticism created an insurmountable barrier that led Mike to walk out.

When necessary, it is important for a manager to give criticism to employees. However, the way in which criticism is given is of the utmost importance. Constructive criticism helps improve performance and also provides opportunities for managers and employees to strengthen working relationships.

Action Tools

When criticizing employees, consider the following action tools:

* ✸ Do not criticize your employees in public. Those who do criticize others in public run the risk of losing those individuals, not only as team players but as employees as well.
* ✸ Always think before speaking, especially in giving criticism. Even the most sincere and well-intended criticism can hurt feelings if spoken tactlessly.
* ✸ If you have negative feedback for an employee, save it for a private session. Whether it is an empty conference room, an employee's office, or the cafeteria when not busy, find a private place to discuss with the problem.
* ✸ Remember, do not taint your employees' reputation, as well as your own, by publicly embarrassing them. It's important to give people feedback, but do so in the right place, at the right time.

51

Stopping Sexual Harassment

Case Problem: "The Dirty Note"

"Look at this, Lou. A disgusting, obscene picture left on my desk by someone in this department," said Pam, an angry quality control inspector, to her manager. "I've had it with this department and you! I'm going to employee relations to ask for a transfer or something. I don't know what yet."

"Just hold your horses, Pam, and sit down," ordered Lou, the manufacturing manager. "I'll close the door and we'll talk about it."

After sitting down at his desk, Lou picked up the note that Pam had given him, looked at it and started chuckling. "Come on, Pam, this is pretty good artwork, and besides, where is your sense of humor?" he jested. "You know, boys will be boys, and the guys were just having a bit of fun with you."

"Fun?" exclaimed Pam. "Not at my expense. I won't take it anymore. Six months ago, I was hired to join a professional manufacturing team. Yet since the very beginning, I've been treated like anything but a professional.

"The people around here stop talking when I come into the room. They won't share information with me when I ask. They exclude me from lunches, and they continue to call me 'sweetie' and 'honey' after I've told them it bothers me.

"I know I'm the only woman in the department, but that doesn't give the guys the right to treat me like a second-class citizen."

"O.K., O.K. So what do you want me to do—threaten the guys with discipline?" asked Lou.

"No," replied Pam, "that's not it. All I ever wanted was to be treated like a human being. But apparently this group doesn't have that capability."

Case Analysis

This situation demonstrates the frustrations of a working woman who is being harassed by coworkers because of her gender. Pam has every right to be treated with full respect as a professional in the department.

In this case, Pam had expressed her dissatisfaction to others in the department but failed to bring to a halt the annoying antics, which culminated in the immature and humiliating dirty picture. Lou's pacifying comments such as "boys will be boys" clearly indicate the manufacturing manager's endorsement of sexual harassment within this department.

Action Tools

To effectively deal with the issue of sexual harassment in the workplace, consider the following action tools:

* Obtain and review your company's sexual harassment policy. This document should include a zero tolerance statement, a clear definition of sexual harassment, examples of prohibited behaviors, a complaint procedure, a procedure for prompt and confidential follow-up and investigation, sanctions that could be taken, and protection against retaliation.
* Publicize the sexual harassment policy by clearly displaying it on bulletin boards and in employee manuals and publications and by discussing it in meetings, employee orientations, and training sessions.
* Promote a sexual harassment-free work environment by personally demonstrating genuine respect for all individuals. Your personal leadership, actions, and words

may help prevent sexual harassment from occurring in the first place.

★ Define sexual harassment as unwelcome and unwanted offensive behavior that emphasizes the gender or sexual identity of an individual.

★ Point out to your employees that this is intimidating and illegal workplace behavior that elicits feelings of fear, guilt, shame, anger, and humiliation.

★ Explain that sexual harassment damages morale, undermines employment relationships, interferes with the work effectiveness of its victims, and robs individuals of their peace of mind and freedom to do their jobs as effectively as possible.

★ Give examples of sexual harassment as persistent pressure, requests or demands for sexual encounters or favors, physical contact of a lewd nature—such as pinching, patting, fondling, or brushing against another's body—sex-oriented kidding, jokes or verbal abuse or pornographic remarks, actions or pictures.

★ Make it clear that harassers in sexual harassment lawsuits are not the only liable parties. Managers and the company itself can also be held accountable and end up sustaining significant financial losses and public relations damage.

52

Handling the Troublesome Employee

Case Problem: "The Disrupter"

"Craig, this thing has gone far enough," said Alex, the quality control manager, to one of his inspectors who, after eight months on the job, has upset the entire manufacturing operation with his negative attitude and manner. "I thought it was partially the fault of the people you had to work with. I realize that a couple of them can be real pains, but this fourth episode—your fight with Judson—is the straw that breaks the camel's back.

"First it was Hendricks, the second-shift supervisor. All right, everyone has trouble with him, and I appreciated the fact that you said you were just defending our quality control practices. But then you had that big blowup with the engineer. I intervened on your behalf and smoothed over the problem, figuring it was partially due to your inexperience with us.

"Then there was the purchasing agent that you had a run-in with. The whole company was buzzing about that episode. In fact, I got grief from the plant manager because of that. I told you then and will repeat again: You can't go around bossing others just because you may be in the right. There are proper ways to work with people and get the results you want.

"But now, Craig, yesterday's shouting match with Judson, our production manager, is totally unacceptable to me. I know Judson to be a highly professional manager. I wouldn't have believed this incident except for the fact that I saw it for myself. Your behavior was uncalled for, totally out of line and highly antagonistic."

Case Analysis

In this case, Alex, the quality control manager, takes a positive stand by confronting an employee who has displayed negative interpersonal behavior toward several individuals in the company. Craig's antagonistic and tactless behavior has brought the image of quality control to an all-time low.

Sometimes employees with negative attitudes and poor interpersonal skills are allowed to go unchecked, disrupt work routines, and foster poor relations in and out of their departments. Such attitudes and behavior should not be tolerated.

When an individual's behavior is found to be destructive to a team effort, the manager has the responsibility to confront the employee exhibiting such behavior and seek rectification of the problem. The fact is that some disruptive employees may not be aware of their own antagonistic tendencies and may never have learned the rules and skills for effective team play.

Action Tools

When an employee's behavior is disruptive to your team or organization, consider the following action tools:

* With facts in hand, talk with the disruptive individual and seek resolution of the problem.
* Have the employee attend training programs that teach the principles and skills of effective human relations, communication, and teamwork.
* Register the employee for an assertiveness training workshop. This can be particularly helpful to individuals who display aggressive tendencies or allow themselves to be easily victimized by others.
* Consider professional counseling for employees who may not be showing any improvement through your other efforts.
* Consult with your manager, human resources representative, or employee assistance program specialist to obtain help and suggestions in dealing with the disruptive employee.

53

Controlling Telephone Abuses

Case Problem: "Phone Home"

Stan, the manufacturing engineering manager, and Clark, the administrative manager, are discussing an excessive phone-usage problem in manufacturing engineering.

"Yeah, it looks pretty evident to me according to your printout, Clark, that all the excessive calls recorded in my area are coming from Marta's line," said Stan.

"Isn't Marta the best engineer you have in your department?" asked Clark.

"Sure, she's the best," replied Stan. "But you can't let things like this go by. And I won't make exceptions even for a top performer. Don't worry, Clark, I'll handle this problem immediately. I don't like people taking advantage of me."

"Stan, just because these bills arc coming from Marta's line doesn't necessarily mean she's making the calls," commented Clark, who sensed a bit of animosity. "Do you see her on the phone all the time?"

"No—her desk isn't near my office," responded Stan, "but I do know she has got school-age kids and a sick, elderly mother. I just know she's talking with them."

"Look, Stan," reasoned Clark, "before you convict the woman, shouldn't you ask her if she's the one making the calls and, if she is, what her reasons are? Give her a chance to explain. Who knows, maybe someone else is using her line. Or you may find she's doing a lot more company business by telephone than you're giving her credit for."

Case Analysis

As Clark suggested, Stan should present the facts in this case to Marta and ask her to account for the excessive phone charges. By doing this, Stan will learn whether Marta is the caller in all cases.

If she is not the caller, then Stan should solicit her help in identifying the true caller(s). If she is the caller, then Stan owes it to her to remind her of company policy on telephone use and then find out the reasons for her excessive use of the telephone.

As Stan's top manufacturing engineer, Marta may have very good business reasons for the extra calls, or Stan may discover that phone calls for personal reasons are needed at this time for emergencies at home.

Whatever the case, Stan has a responsibility to the company and to Marta to present a questioning and helpful approach to solving the problem and to avoid prejudgments, condemnation, and premature discipline. With this type of positive problem-solving approach, Stan has a greater chance of gaining Marta's support and solving the problem successfully.

Action Tools

To effectively deal with telephone abuse, consider the following action tools:

- ✱ Communicate rules for phone use as part of department orientation.
- ✱ When you note telephone overuse, make sure you present the facts objectively to the party suspected.
- ✱ Allow the individual an opportunity to clear him/herself and provide an explanation for the phone excess.
- ✱ If the phone is being used excessively for personal reasons, explain the need for adherence to telephone rules, but be flexible in working out some way to assist an employee at a time of personal need.

54

Leveling With People to Reduce Conflict

Case Problem: "Over Your Head"

"Politics, politics, I know what politics are," thought Ted, the industrial relations manager. "I've got this employee who thinks absolutely nothing of going over my head to the new division manager to get some quick answers. "What's worse is that my new manager seems to like it. He thinks he's got an open-door policy. What he has is an open-door brain!

"Yesterday, the division manager went right past my office to give a few of my people some assignments. They stopped everything for him and got behind on my top priorities. I wish he had come to me first or, at least, had informed me of his actions.

"I feel like the monkey in the middle. I just don't know what to do. I thought I had a team, but we no longer seem to work like one. I just can't handle it; but I'm afraid that if I tell my people to cut it out, I'll look bad to my boss."

Case Analysis

Ted, the industrial relations manager, is justly concerned about the new behavior and habits of an employee as well as the behavior of his new manager. It is apparent to Ted that his employee and boss are violating the chain of command and undermining the departmental team by regularly bypassing him when they should be working through and with him.

This situation requires frank discussion. Ted's goal is to build a "win-win situation" with his new manager as well as to reaffirm his leadership role with his staff. Ted must act now to prevent any further problems down the road.

He must level with his manager and with his employee individually and in private. He must assert himself tactfully and professionally, explain what is troubling him, and help develop a course of action to get the team back on track.

Action Tools

To effectively confront and resolve a performance problem, the following steps should be taken:

- ✴ Decide to deal with the problem as soon as possible. Consider the problem, some of its possible causes, and even some possible solutions. Then, approach the person involved in a calm but serious manner.
- ✴ Hold your meeting in private in a comfortable setting that allows for maximum openness of communication.
- ✴ Describe the problem in specific terms, providing as much factual data as possible. Avoid small talk. Instead, get right to the problem.
- ✴ Should you feel personal disappointment with the employee or know of negative consequences resulting from the performance problem, you may share these feelings and facts. However, be careful to do so in a nonthreatening and nonaccusatory manner.
- ✴ Ask the individual what happened, why, and how it can be resolved. Then listen!
- ✴ Help reduce any defensiveness on the part of the listener by reaffirming your positive relationship and confidence in the individual.
- ✴ Do not talk about other problems in this meeting. Keep your discussion centered on the problem at hand.
- ✴ Arrive at a mutually agreeable solution and confirm that decision with a handshake.

55

Resolving Conflicts Through Mediation

Case Problem: "A Split in the Ranks"

How would you feel if your manager called you on the carpet and told you he didn't approve of the way you were operating your department? Such was the case for Jack, the accounting manager of Cowbar International, who was shaken by the comments of his manager, Ken.

"You have a problem, Jack," said Ken, the controller. "Every department knows about the armed camps in your area. You have known ringleaders who seem to call all the shots around here. Your staff is making me look bad. I'm getting all kinds of negative feedback from people in other departments."

"Hold on," responded Jack, defensively. "I do my work, and my people get the job done. I'm not paid to be a cop. I stay out of their way. I tell them what to do and let them do it. How they get it done is their business, not mine."

"Well, we'll see about that in your upcoming performance review, Mr. Know-It-All," said Ken. "And even if productivity were high, which isn't the case, your employees' behavior inside this department and throughout the company is your responsibility. And you will definitely be reviewed on that count.

"Look, Jack," continued Ken, "I know there is an ongoing dispute between two of your key people, and the rest of your department is split down the center. This dispute has to stop. You can't beg off this one any longer. For your own good, handle this now."

Case Analysis

In this situation, there is a continuing dispute between two accountants that has divided the ranks of the accounting department. The accounting manager, who is either afraid of his own people or honestly believes his actions are appropriate, keeps out of the dispute. But his "hands-off" policy backfires, resulting in a censure from his manager.

The fact is that maintaining harmonious relations and helping resolve interpersonal disputes are important responsibilities of an effective manager. It is therefore appropriate that in Jack's upcoming review, Ken, the controller, will have something serious to say about Jack's inability to control interpersonal conflict and maintain harmony among the staff.

Action Tools

To effectively mediate conflict within your department, consider the following action tools:

* Intervene firmly but tactfully when confronted with warring individuals or groups reporting to you.
* Let them know you will act as a mediator in helping them talk through their problems and work out agreeable solutions.
* Indicate that you care about them and that a satisfactory solution must be worked out for their mutual benefit as well as for peace and harmony within the department.
* Bring both parties together in a closed room or private area.
* Establish clear ground rules for communicating in the meeting. For example, the parties in conflict may not speak to each other at any time, and all communications must be with and through you.
* Acting as mediator, help your employees get both versions of their problem out on the table. Do not allow one disputant to interrupt while the other is speaking.

✷ Once both parties come to agreement on the same version of the problem, begin the search for a mutually satisfactory solution. State in your ground rules that only one party at a time can propose solutions or amend previous proposals until an agreement is reached.

✷ In very difficult situations, exercise your authority as manager and lay down the law. Enforce your meeting ground rules, and if necessary, enforce a truce between the warring parties.

56

Administering Discipline

Case Problem: "A Lack of Discipline"

"What a joke for a boss," remarked Tim, a sales representative, to his friend Amanda, a production planner, as they chatted over lunch. "Charlie, my sales manager, has been in his position only one year; and in that short time, he has earned the department title of 'Charlie Chicken.'"

"How come?" asked Amanda.

"The guy's a dud," replied Tim. "No backbone, no guts. You see, last year when Barry left the company, they gave Charlie the job because he was a top seller and was an O.K. guy, too."

"So, what's wrong with those qualifications?" asked Amanda.

"Nothing especially," said Tim. "I guess being a top producer and pretty well liked are good qualities for a manager. It's just that he can't handle problems when they come up. I mean, when certain sales or support staff abuse rules and violate important policies, he just lets these people get away with it.

"It drives me up the wall because some people continually get away with it, while guys like me and Rudy are trying to do our best. We end up looking like the fools."

"What is it about Charlie that makes him so soft on discipline?" asked Amanda.

"I think there are two basic problems," replied Tim. "First, Charlie was selling for five years before the promotion. He's friendly with a number of the folks here. I think he's afraid to discipline his friends for fear he'll lose their friendship."

"And what's the second reason?" inquired Amanda.

"The guy is scared of a couple of the people," replied Tim. "I mean he's literally intimidated by Swenson, who's a big, tough-looking fellow—six feet five inches—and by Barbara, who is a personal friend of Ella, our national sales manager.

"But come to think of it," added Tim, "I think he's also afraid of taking disciplinary action because so many employee complaints from other departments have been filed with the company grievance committee and disciplinary decisions have been overturned."

"Well," said Amanda, "I can understand that kind of fear, especially since Owen, the manufacturing superintendent, is the cause for many of the grievances filed in the first place."

"Yeah. I've heard about his reputation," remarked Tim. "I hear he just looks for opportunities to get you people."

"You've heard right," agreed Amanda. "Just in the last month alone, he discharged a guy, put two people on suspension, and wrote up four others. In fact, one of the guys he suspended is our very best machinist. And what's really unfair is the guy didn't do anything that bad. It's something that's generally done around here by all of us but has never been criticized."

"That's unreal, Amanda," said Tim. "How do you folks get anything done around here? Sounds as though manufacturing is more involved in fighting than in getting the work out."

"Our performance is way down," admitted Amanda. "But I'll tell you a little secret: Several of us are not taking Owen's injustices anymore. We've decided to make it as tough on him as he's making it on us. There's only one way to get him, and that's by reducing our own efforts and getting a little sloppy. Then you'll see the big brass start coming down on him fast enough."

As the friends were commiserating about their managers, Eric, a new equipment operator of only four months, walked over and sat down.

"What's wrong, Eric?" asked Tim, pointing at Eric's trembling hands. "You're all red in the face. What happened?"

"I just came from Owen's office," explained Eric, "And boy, did he let me have it."

"For what?" asked Amanda.

"I'm not really sure," responded Eric, appearing extremely upset. "He charged me with so many different crimes I can't recall any of them now."

"Be more specific. What did he say?" asked Amanda.

"He said something about tardiness and loafing on the job," replied Eric, "and accused me of negligence and insubordination, even stealing. Honestly, I had no idea what he was talking about.

"All I know is that the guy said he's writing me up. He also threatened me with suspension. What will I do? All I wanted was to do a great job and have my boss respect me."

As Eric's last words were spoken, the group overheard yelling coming from the hallway in front of the cafeteria:

"Bob, you are about the stupidest person I know." It was Owen, the superintendent, shouting in an angry voice at his administrative assistant, Bob, a very competent and friendly individual. "You do that again and you can kiss this job goodbye."

"You see, Eric," stated Amanda, "you're not alone. That guy threatens all of us the same. You might say he's consistently unfair."

Case Analysis

In this case, two managers have special problems in handling discipline. The sales manager, called "Charlie Chicken" by the sales staff, is incapable of mustering the strength and confidence to dispense necessary discipline in the face of clear violations of rules and regulations by certain salespeople. His failure to dole out justice appropriately takes its toll by destroying his credibility among the conscientious employees.

The manufacturing superintendent presents considerably different problems. He is preoccupied with finding fault and administering discipline—often not justified—to the detriment of productivity and staff harmony.

The employees in manufacturing are, in turn, preoccupied with negative feelings of defensiveness, formal grievances, even acts of sabotage. Inequity, injustice, and the thoughtless use of power characterize this boss bent on the unreasonable domination and control of manufacturing.

Action Tools

To effectively carry out the responsibility for fair and just discipline, a manager should consider the following action tools:

✸ Encourage each employee to assume personal responsibility for adhering to organizational rules and regulations and for self-development and self-improvement when not in conformity.

★ Never blindly assume an employee's guilt or negative intentions if policies or rules are violated. Instead, investigate any charges and collect supporting evidence. Then, if the charge is verified, present it to the employee with the goal of understanding its causes and seeking appropriate correction.

★ Make certain the staff understands the negative disciplinary system that is occasionally needed to assure employee conformance with important organizational standards. This understanding can be achieved through group discussions of various company rules and policies and by allowing department members to voice feelings and opinions about the importance of such guides and the occasional need for appropriate punitive action.

★ Attempt to prevent the need for excessive negative discipline by more effective recruiting, selection, orientation, and training. Extra care in these management areas can help reduce the need for dispensing negative discipline later.

★ Be perceived as a fair-minded manager who can reward superior performance but who can also administer necessary discipline.

★ Understand the various forms of negative discipline that are prescribed. In addition, understand your authority to make and carry out these disciplinary decisions. Should you handle a problem independently or in conjunction with higher authorities? Be cautious to avoid making an independent decision to discipline an employee if joint decision-making is required. Such mistakes damage a manager's credibility.

★ Administer appropriate disciplinary measures based upon the severity of a problem, frequency of a violation, and history or prior disciplinary pattern of an employee.

★ Be fair and consistent in carrying out the procedure of negative discipline. Understand that unfair and inconsistent punishment of employees is a major cause of employee complaints and grievances.

✦ Be certain to accurately document all disciplinary discussions and decisions. This ensures that groups inquiring about the procedure used—be they union or nonunion groups, grievance bodies, or government agencies—can be fully informed through clear records of the events.

57

Managing Conflict in Urgent Situations

Case Problem: "The Short Trip"

More than 5,000 sales associates and managers of a diversified financial services company are converging on Boston from around the country. This is their twenty-fifth anniversary meeting, and anyone who is anyone will be there.

It is now 7:30 AM on Monday, and the participants are leaving their hotels, going over to the convention center where the kick-off meeting will begin at 8:30 AM The president of the company will be the lead speaker.

Larry, a sales manager from Detroit, and Bob, a sales manager from Chicago, are staying at a hotel about two blocks from the entrance of the convention center. Each manager has brought with him heavy boxes containing hand-outs for the morning session.

At the hotel entrance, a bellman hails the next cab in the taxi line, and the cab drives up to the pick-up area. The bellman places the heavy cartons into the trunk and helps the two managers into the cab.

"Where to?" the cab driver asks. Larry responds, "The convention center main entrance, please."

"I've waited an hour in this line, and you're sticking me with this short trip?" the cab driver asks angrily. "The convention center is across the street. Why don't you walk?"

"Don't you raise your voice at us," reacts Larry. "Just take us to the convention center, or we'll be late."

"The bellman shouldn't have put you in my cab," responds the cab driver. "He knew you were a short trip, and he's trying to be a big shot. Just get out of my cab!"

"Look, you'd better take us over to the convention center, or we'll call the police," threatens Larry.

"Oh, yeah?" responds the driver. "Go ahead and call the cops. Just get out of my cab now so I can get a real ride!"

Seeing the argument escalate, Bob appeals, "Sir, please forgive my friend. We are both really sorry for the inconvenience to you and don't understand the taxi system in Boston. We have heavy boxes in your trunk and must get over to the convention center in a hurry.

"At the airports, cab drivers who get short trips usually receive passes that allow them to come back to the front of the taxi line when returning to the airports. Isn't it the same here at the hotels?"

"No," responds the cab driver. "That's only at the airports."

To resolve the situation, Bob offers, "Sir, if you take us to the center, I'll give you a big tip, O.K.?"

The cab driver agrees and drives the men to the entrance of the convention center. The meter flashes $2.75. Bob hands the driver a ten dollar bill and tells him to "Keep the change." The driver looks at the bill and immediately starts apologizing for his behavior, thanking the men. He quickly jumps out of the cab, removes the boxes from the trunk, and helps the two men carry the boxes into the building.

Case Analysis

Here a seemingly simple activity—taking a cab—unexpectedly turns into a heated argument. The two sales managers, who are desperately trying to get to their meeting on time, meet up with a cab driver who believes he is being exploited by the hotel bellman and unfair passengers.

What to do? Larry uses the direct approach, telling the cab driver to do his job and to lower his voice. He even threatens the driver with calling the police. This strong and direct approach, however, does not work and actually increases the level of conflict.

Quickly assessing the situation, Bob realizes that Larry's approach will result in their being ejected from the cab and possibly being late to their important meeting. Bob knows that time is of the essence and that this cab may be their only chance to arrive at the convention center on time.

He senses that the driver is genuinely upset and decides to approach the situation from a different perspective. First, he acknowledges the driver's frustration and expresses his sympathy for the driver's plight. Next, he inquires about taxi protocol at the Boston hotels. Finally, Bob assures the driver that he will give him a big tip for his inconvenience.

The result: The sales managers are driven to their destination quickly and treated with courtesy in the process.

Given all the facts in this urgent situation, including the managers' need to get to the convention center quickly and the cab driver's feeling of exploitation, it appears that the calmer, empathetic and motivating approach was the appropriate response to achieve the needed win-win situation.

Action Tools

Don't be surprised when your positive expectations of the people who work with you are not always fulfilled.

If you are suddenly let down, disappointed, or obstructed by those you depend upon, consider the following action tools:

- Temporarily set aside your own needs, and change your "emotional channel" from that of angry victim to counselor.
- Try to understand the other's situation and acknowledge any underlying frustrations.
- Then, if still appropriate, ask for the individual's help, explain your predicament, and offer any assistance possible to help motivate the action.

Section VIII

Employee Development

58

Succession Planning

Case Problem: "The Chosen One"

Tim, the plant controller at the Tinton plant, had been with the company longer than any of his peers at the other six plants in the division. In addition, his department's accounting achievements were considered tops by plant management as well as divisional executives. At least, that's what he'd been told.

On this evening, upon returning home from the office, Tim walked through the front door, looking depressed and gloomy.

"What's wrong?" asked Sharon, his wife. "You look awful. Oh, I know . . . you didn't get the promotion. Am I right?"

"You've got it right," answered Tim.

Just then, Sharon's brother, Sam, walked into the living room from the kitchen.

"Hi, fella! What's going on?" greeted Sam.

Sharon explained that her brother, a sales manager with a large office supply company, was visiting town on business and was joining them for dinner.

As the three sat down, Tim explained that he had been considered for an accounting executive position at the divisional level, but this afternoon he was notified that another individual got the position instead.

"I'm really sorry. I guess you really wanted that job," said Sam.

"Yes, he did," complained Sharon, "and I don't think that it's fair. Who got it anyway, Tim?"

"Some guy from our plant in Georgia by the name of Carson," replied Tim. "Can you imagine relocating a guy one thousand miles to divisional headquarters here in Tinton when I already live here and work at the Tinton plant? It's crazy!"

"Who's this Carson guy, anyway?" asked Sharon.

"All I can say," said Tim, "is that he's only been with the company seven years, with three years as a plant controller. I've been with the company for fifteen years and have twice the time in as a controller."

"Oh, Tim, I'm so sorry for you," sympathized Sharon. "I just don't understand. Your department record in accounting is unbeatable throughout the company. Everyone knows that. What could the problem be?"

"Well, when I spoke with Paul, our human resources manager, this afternoon, he used the term 'management positioning' to explain the reason. He acknowledged my accounting performance but said the decision had more to do with management development matters."

"That's a lot of bunk!" cried Sharon. "It's all politics. I guess it doesn't really matter how competent a person is or how hard one tries."

"No, Sharon," differed Tim, "perhaps it was partially my fault. As Paul explained it, this Carson fellow didn't have my time in or my accounting record. What he did do that apparently I didn't do was to prepare himself for a promotion."

"But isn't excellence in your job enough? Doesn't the company want loyalty?" asked Sharon.

"I'll bet I know exactly what happened," interrupted Sam. "Carson probably developed an understudy or back-up for himself and you didn't. Am I right?"

"That's partially true," replied Tim. "One of the reasons given to me was that Carson had trained one of his supervisors to serve as assistant or back-up and was preparing the guy to take over the plant controller's job should a promotion come up."

"And you didn't, right?" asked Sam.

"I never thought about it," responded Tim. "And furthermore, replacements, back-ups, successors—no one ever mentioned these things to me before. Anyway, when the honchos at divisional had to make the decision, they went with Carson because, as Paul explained, promoting me would have left an organizational hole in accounting at the Tinton plant and would have interrupted accounting operations.

"By promoting Carson, instead the company would assure operational continuity in Georgia because the replacement would be able to immediately take over the controllership there."

"What about your relationship with headquarters?" inquired Sam.

"It's interesting you should ask that," said Tim. "Paul also said that my relationship with headquarters had a lot to do with the decision. Apparently, Carson had been working with the vice president at headquarters on a division-wide accounting task force and also assisted the guy who quit on some special projects."

"That sounds about right," said Sam. "In other words, Carson was getting company-wide exposure and developing himself as a possible successor to the guy who left while you were doing your job as controller at the plant level."

"Yup, but to be totally fair," explained Tim, "Carson's accounting operation was being handled effectively. I mean, he wasn't goofing off in his job. It's just that his assistant apparently gave him more time to work on his own career development as well."

Case Analysis

Promotions to higher management positions are often rewards for those managers who plan their own career development concurrent with the development of their staff. For those managers who seek promotion, current job excellence is certainly important, but, by itself, simply not enough.

As a manager is considered for promotion, two important questions are asked:

1. Does the manager have the potential to assume the new responsibilities as well as some proven skills and background in the new position?
2. Does the manager have one or more trained and trusted successors to immediately assume his or her responsibilities should the promotion be offered?

If both questions are answered in the affirmative, the manager can successfully be promoted without creating an organizational hole in the department and thereby interrupting the flow of operations.

It is sad that Tim learned the secrets of career development too late for this promotional opportunity. It is also sad that Tim's plant manager, human resources manager, or executives at divisional headquarters failed to acquaint him with opportunities for management development in the company. But the ultimate responsibility for his career success was his own.

Action Tools

To be seriously considered for promotion to higher-level management positions, consider the following tips:

* Assume personal responsibility for your own career plan.
* Speak with superiors and arrange for developmental opportunities that will position you for possible future openings.
* Identify one or more aspiring and competent subordinates who can be trained as your potential replacement or successor. Such persons, once fully developed, can also be recommended for alternative management spots elsewhere in the company.
* Recognize the mutual benefits to be derived by the company and you, the manager, by promoting capable and aspiring individuals from within.

59

Developing Your Staff

Case Problem: "The Undeveloped Staff"

Sam, the manager of equipment design for a mid-sized company, says he doesn't believe in training his staff. Moreover, he says there's enough good talent in the marketplace when needs arise. He refuses to develop anyone on his staff for advancement and feels it's a waste of company time and money. Besides, he says, people just want the easy life.

But Sam's ears must have been burning yesterday when, in the company's coffee room, two of his design engineers were engaged in a heated conversation about his policy.

"I just can't take it anymore!" said Murray to his colleague, Maria. "I'm sick and tired of Sam treating me as if I don't exist.

"Doesn't that guy see that I'm good at what I do? Doesn't he know I want to move ahead in the company? He actually seems to want to hold me back.

"I remember when Sam used to like to give me responsibilities; in fact, he encouraged me so he would have time to do other things. But that didn't last. Ever since the 'big brass' told me, in front of him, that I was doing a terrific job, he's been holding back on those good jobs and having me do all the junk work."

"I know just what you're talking about," commiserated Maria. "I, too, am concerned about my future here. I've asked him for some training and extra responsibilities, but he just ignores me, as if my career needs are unimportant. From the way he acts, you'd think I wanted his job. Come to think of it, that's not a bad idea!"

Case Analysis

Too bad Sam didn't hear this conversation. If he had, he might have realized that failure to develop employees frequently produces a domino effect. In this situation, Sam's employees are utterly frustrated because he has refused to recognize their career needs and provide development opportunities. As a result, they are turning to each other—and against him—for solace.

Professional development and career advancement are important goals to many employees. Therefore, it is necessary for managers to recognize those individuals who possess strong career aspirations and work with them in achieving their goals.

Such a commitment to employee development fosters employee initiative and loyalty and provides a pool of qualified talent for future organizational needs.

Action Tools

To effectively develop your staff, consider the following action tools:

* Sit down with your staff members individually to identify their professional aspirations and career goals. Remember, it is important to line up a possible successor so you can move up, should you desire.
* Delegate higher-level responsibilities to capable individuals who show a desire to advance. Remember to give appropriate authority to them so they will be able to get the job done.
* Follow up on a regular basis to see how your staff members are handling their career development assignments.
* Give your employees regular feedback on their progress in reaching their career goals.

60

Developing Your Management Career Path

Case Problem: "Bored Bentley"

"I'm so tired and bored, Jeff," said Bentley, the safety supervisor. "It seems like the days last forever around here. I want to be energetic and happy at work, but it's becoming an uphill climb lately."

"Relax," advised Jeff, a friend from the human resources department. "It's the end of the summer, and it's just plain hot and miserable. Everyone feels a little lazy and low now."

"No, Jeff, that's not it at all," responded Bentley. "I really feel like I'm going absolutely nowhere with my job and my career."

"Well, Bentley, have you ever shared your feelings with Sara, your manager?" asked Jeff. "She's a terrific person and would probably like to hear what you're telling me right now."

"I know she's terrific," Bentley responded, "and we really work well together. It's just that she's been so good to me, I really wouldn't want to appear ungrateful, dissatisfied, or greedy."

"If you're really frustrated," said Jeff, "and feel down in the dumps with no sense of career direction at this company, you'd better sit down with her and discuss your needs and plans for the future.

"Bentley, you're not doing yourself or her any good by keeping it pent up inside you. It's going to show up in one way or another; and the fact of the matter is, your silence about your frustrations will probably be misinterpreted. She may even think you don't care about the company and peg you as a loser."

Case Analysis

Frequently, individuals hesitate to share their needs and frustrations with their managers, fearing they may appear ungrateful and selfish. But not leveling with a manager about important personal concerns produces a no-win situation for both parties: the one who remains frustrated and the manager who remains unaware of the problems.

In this case, Bentley should take the initiative in getting out of his rut and on to a career path. He simply cannot expect his manager to be aware of all his personal problems and desires unless he is willing to trust and communicate them to her.

Action Tools

To further advance your management career and prevent boredom and stagnation in your current job, consider this five-step process:

★ Take the initiative and discuss your career needs with your immediate supervisor.

★ Solicit his/her cooperation in the development and support of a career plan.

★ Prepare a career plan by writing down on a sheet of paper where you see yourself in your career in one year, two years, and five years from now.

★ Consider and then write down how you are going to achieve your career goals (college, technical classes, seminars, on-the-job training, certificates, etc.).

★ Set milestones or progress checkpoints to assure that you play out your strategy.

61

Developing Employee Interest and Potential

Case Problem: "The Awakening"

Matt, a quiet sensitive purchasing assistant had been working for about two years at his present job. Before joining the company, he had spent two years in procurement in the Army, with one of those years as a supervisor. Yet, in his present job, Matt had been pegged as a detail man by Ralph, the purchasing manager, who was an autocratic boss with little concern for his staff's personal needs or professional potential.

Without knowing very much about his people's goals or capabilities, Ralph gave his boss, Al, the director of materials management, the strong impression that Matt was not a "people person" or management material. Until this time, the director had simply accepted as accurate Ralph's impressions about the purchasing staff. Since the work was getting done on time, there seemed to be no reason for the director to doubt Ralph's word.

This week, however, during a plant-wide professional development meeting, the director was getting feedback from an outside consultant who was leading one of the development workshops.

"Al, it looks like you've got some real management potential in your organization," said the consultant. "I especially feel that Matt, a purchasing assistant, displays superior ability for management. I sure hope you've got him pegged for some future management slot."

Looking puzzled, the director replied, "Are you sure we're talking about the same guy? This is the first I've heard about Matt's ability. In fact, his manager has assured me that Matt had no interest or potential at all in management. I just don't understand."

Case Analysis

It is clear from this case that the director did not know his purchasing manager as well as he thought. A false assumption had been made by the director that good purchasing results meant the purchasing staff was being given sufficient chance for self-expression and personal development. He had also incorrectly assumed that the information about the staff that was communicated upstairs by the purchasing manager was accurate.

The purchasing manager was unfair to his purchasing assistant as well as to the company by misinforming the director about the desires and abilities of this individual without having any real information on the subject. In fact, the purchasing manager never inquired about Matt's interest in management, never acknowledged Matt's experience as a procurement supervisor in the Army, and never attempted to test Matt's ability in a management back-up situation.

Action Tools

In today's demanding business environment, employee development has become a major competitive advantage for the most successful organizations. By encouraging employees to continuously increase their skills and knowledge, managers help prevent employee obsolescence and enhance employee value within the company and marketplace.

To help you become more effective in developing your people, consider the following action tools:

- ✳ Commit to pursuing employee development as a key management strategy for maintaining high performance and achieving business objectives.
- ✳ Work closely with your manager and other members of your management team to raise awareness of the im-

portance of employee development, and create an environment that encourages and rewards it.

★ Get agreement between you and your manager to include employee development as an important performance expectation within your own annual performance plan.

★ Meet with each of your employees to create annual performance plans. As part of this process, clearly spell out your performance expectations and priorities. In addition, solicit employee interests and desires for professional and career development. Encourage employees to take the lead in identifying and carrying out training and development activities to meet performance expectations.

★ Meet with employees on an ongoing basis to provide feedback on their performance and coaching whenever appropriate.

★ Keep your manager informed of each employee's performance development plans and progress.

62

Cultivating the Seasoned Employee

Case Problem: "Looking Back"

Josh, a 61-year-old customer service specialist, was sitting at his desk thinking about his job.

"I feel so wasted," he thought. "What is it all about? All these years I've spent in this company, and they treat me like a child. They placate me. How insulting.

"I've been here more than thirty-five years. All these new people. . . . Where did they come from? Why, Max hasn't been here five years, and he has gotten all kinds of promotions and bucks—the kinds I wish I'd have gotten when I was his age. It'll be a cold day when I volunteer any of my hard earned 'secrets' to him."

Suddenly, startled by the phone, Josh picked up the receiver.

"What do you mean you don't like the way the survey is proceeding? What do you know?" reacted Josh to a peer who was working with him on a customer research project. "I've been doing this since before you were born. Don't tell me what I'm doing wrong."

Josh sank back into thought as he stared at the clock on his desk.

"I helped build this place, but they don't care. It seems so strange when I look around sometimes. What was it that punk said to me under his breath? 'Old man?' Well, maybe I am old. I'm certainly tired. Perhaps bored is more the case. I'm not going anywhere—that's for sure."

Case Analysis

Disappointment, fear, realization of a future never to come—such are the plights of many senior employees. Josh is such an employee caught in this trap. He is, in his own mind, isolated from the very company he had helped to build. Within the changing surroundings of his company, Josh is sensitive to the manner in which he is being treated. This has paralyzed his energies.

He is anxious and perhaps envious of Max's promotions. He can only think of how he wished he had been more ambitious in his younger days. These feelings, too, immobilize his ability to deal with his colleagues, his company, and himself.

Action Tools

Develop your senior/seasoned employees by taking the following actions:

- Keep the seasoned employee as a vital part of your team to enliven his/her commitment to the organization.
- Continue to reaffirm the company's belief in and commitment to its seasoned and loyal people.
- Have the seasoned employee assist you in training and guiding new staff members.
- Cultivate the senior employee as a possible staff and supervisory back-up.
- Solicit the senior employee's help on special projects. Remember, this individual has many years of in-depth experience with the company and, if properly utilized, can contribute valuable insights, respected leadership, and genuine enthusiasm to your team's efforts.

63

Encouraging Continual Learning and Improvement

Case Problem: "The Saga of Ripley Van Winkle"

After completing a workshop in New York City, Dr. Heinrich Becker, the director of quality control for a major pharmaceutical company, hailed a taxi to go to the airport for his flight home. As he entered the cab, he recognized an old friend at the wheel.

"Ripley, Ripley Van Winkle, is it you?" he asked. "Are you Ripley Van Winkle, my old classmate from MIT?"

The driver turned around to look at his passenger and saw the face of his old friend, Heinrich.

"Heinrich Becker!" he exclaimed, "I can't believe it! It's me, Ripley. I haven't seen you in years!"

Fifteen years earlier, the two men had done their graduate work in chemistry together at MIT and graduated with their Ph.D.s at the top of their class. Now, by chance, they met in a New York City yellow cab and renewed their acquaintance.

Ripley suggested that Heinrich and he have dinner together at the airport while waiting for Heinrich's plane. There was plenty of time before Heinrich's flight was scheduled to depart. They agreed.

Over dinner, the two brought each other up to date on their lives and careers. Heinrich had worked in pharmaceuticals all these years and was now the director of quality control and doing well. Ripley had taken a staff scientist position in the food industry, and five years ago he had been promoted to director of analytical services for a large diversified food company.

Heinrich was confused.

"Ripley, how come you're driving a taxi now? What about your management position?" he inquired.

"One day, around two years ago, I went to work and without any warning, it's all over!" Ripley explained. "There, on my desk, was a memo from the vice president of research and development announcing that our entire department had been outsourced to some independent lab. Can you believe that . . . and without any warning?"

"Oh, I'm so sorry that happened to you, my friend," reacted Heinrich, sympathetically. "But why are you driving a taxi? Why aren't you working in your field?"

Ripley explained that he had tried to get another similar position for several months, but with no success. And, last year, in order to put food on the table, he leased this taxi.

"I put in twelve to fifteen hours each day, six days a week, and make a pretty good living," said Ripley. "It's very hard work, and I'm grateful to be able to work. But it's not really what I would prefer."

As Heinrich listened, he recalled a speech he had heard.

"Ripley, around four years ago, I heard a Dr. Frederick Margolis give a presentation at a national conference in Chicago. He was your vice president, wasn't he?" asked Heinrich. "Yes, he was," responded Ripley. "What was he talking about?"

"You won't believe this," answered Heinrich. "Cost-saving business strategies in science and technology. And he seemed to emphasize outsourcing as his preferred method."

Ripley listened intently as Heinrich continued.

"Your vice president even shared some of his own plans to consider outsourcing some of his own functions in your old company. And that was around four years ago."

As Ripley listened, he wondered why Margolis hadn't mentioned these plans inside the company.

"And the strangest thing," Heinrich continued, "around the same time, my vice president, Tom Glover, made a formal announcement at our company that our president had just asked each business unit president, as well as Tom, to review each of our functions for possible outsourcing. The word was that, after about one year, any department that could be outsourced and that could not compete with a comparable outsourcing firm, measure for measure, would be eliminated."

"That's incredible!" reacted Ripley. "If we had only known Margolis's intentions at our company. At least you received some advance warning."

"As you can imagine," Heinrich added, "Everybody at our company started learning new ways to cut costs, raise quality, improve teamwork and speed up turnaround time. Some of the departments succeeded and are still in place, while others failed miserably and are gone."

"What did you do?" asked Ripley.

"Fortunately for us," continued Heinrich, "A few years earlier, I had, on my own initiative, started to benchmark other organizations, including independent labs. I learned what we needed to do, and we did it. So by the time our president made his announcement, the numbers in Quality Control were far ahead of any possible threat. We were safe."

"Congratulations, Heinrich, you're so smart. You were miles ahead," praised Ripley.

"You know," added Heinrich, "it was in all the magazines that I was getting: total quality, downsizing, continuous improvement, reengineering, outsourcing. And Margolis and Glover weren't the first to make me aware of these trends. They talk about this stuff at our monthly association meetings and workshops that I attend. I just couldn't miss it.

"But what about you, Ripley? Are you sure Margolis never mentioned it in your company?"

"Not that I was aware of," claimed Ripley. "Of course, I had missed several of the management staff meetings because of the pressures in our department. trying to get the work out, you know."

"But hadn't friends in the company mentioned anything to you?" asked Heinrich.

"Friends, I had no friends there," explained Ripley. "I didn't really get along with the other directors, and I didn't spend much time with them."

"But shouldn't you have been aware that all these changes were coming?" asked Heinrich. "Aren't you a member of The Chemical Society and its local chapter?"

"No, not really," answered Ripley. "I was a member for two years, but then stopped attending meetings. I knew all that stuff anyway—just a bunch of chemists standing around, tooting their own horns. I had real work to do back at the lab."

"And what about your spare time after work?" asked Heinrich. "Did you read about these things and how they are changing our workplace?"

"No," admitted Ripley. "I guess I didn't. I just spent all my spare time relaxing, trying to forget work, to just get away from it all and to reduce some of the daily pressures."

Heinrich noticed the clock on the wall and saw that his flight would be leaving in just half an hour, so he said goodbye to his old friend.

"Look, Ripley, I've got to go now. It was great seeing you. Just remember this: It's a new world now. Everything is changing from day to day. Nothing remains the same. When you do land a position that you want, remember to stay on top of things. Stay ahead of the game. Don't be the last to find out. Be the first to know. And use that information to improve your situation, O.K.?"

The two men exchanged goodbyes, and Heinrich was off.

"Heinrich is right," Ripley thought. "I was in a rut, always doing the same job the same way. From now on, it'll be different. I'll start improving myself today.

"Maybe I'll go out and buy a map of New York City. I'll bet there are all kinds of shortcuts I can find to get my passengers to their destinations more quickly. That's how the London cab drivers do it."

Case Analysis

In this case, we meet two individuals: Dr. Ripley Van Winkle and Dr. Heinrich Becker. Both are extremely well educated, at the top of their class, and high achievers.

While both men have similar backgrounds with seemingly great career potential in their chosen fields, only Heinrich had discovered a truth that is a requirement for success in today's rapidly changing business environment: continual learning and improvement. From their conversations, we realize that Ripley Van Winkle, as his name suggests, fell asleep on the job, letting a world of new knowledge and opportunity pass him by. And upon awakening, he discovered that his department's function was now being carried out by an outsourcing firm and that he was unemployed.

When he was director of analytical services, Ripley concerned himself exclusively with the present, focusing entirely on getting the work out. Unfortunately, he paid no attention to the future, or gaining new knowledge to improve himself, his department, his company, and his life.

Perhaps by this chance meeting with an old schoolmate, Ripley, who by nature is a very hard worker, may have discovered a key success principle: "Do today's job as best you can.

But do tomorrow's job even better by continually searching for new ways, new ideas, and new breakthroughs."

It looks as though Dr. Ripley Van Winkle may soon get back on the right road, whether he's driving a New York City yellow cab or back in the lab.

Action Tools

Commit to a philosophy of continual learning and improvement using the following suggestions:

* Encourage yourself and your employees to value, pursue, and utilize new knowledge, skills, and technologies in current and planned projects and processes.
* Utilize in-company training, university courses, and professional association educational offerings.
* Read department and company-wide communications as well as professional and technical newsletters, reports, journals, and books.
* Keep abreast of new managerial, organizational, and technical developments in your field by networking with company associates and professional colleagues in other companies.
* Attend company meetings to learn about upcoming programs and new initiatives. Also attend professional and technical association meetings to see what's hot and what's not.
* Survey and visit customers to learn about their new and changing needs.
* Keep your eye on suppliers in your field, looking out for new and improved products and services.
* Beware of developing "tunnelvision" by overly focusing your learning in a single technical area. Instead, become familiar with the unfamiliar by joining multidisciplinary teams and by meeting new people from different disciplines.

Section IX

Time and Stress Management

64

Managing the Staff's Time

Case Problem: "Time's A-Wastin'"

"He did it again, he constantly interrupts me," complained Tom, an up-and-coming civil engineer, to his colleague, Jeff.

"What's going on anyway?" asked Jeff.

"It's Ted, our beloved boss," responded Tom. "He has absolutely no regard, no respect for the things I've got to get done in a day. He gives me jobs to do; then, as soon as I become involved in an assignment, he pulls me off of it and sidetracks me with other things. I never have time to finish anything. And when I do get behind in my work, well, it's a sin. Mine!

"Just last week he dragged me out of an important training session to search for a folder that was sitting on his desk. Because of this, I missed an important part of the program and was never able to catch up with the rest of the class. It was embarrassing. This was a program I really wanted to attend."

"I know just what you're talking about," responded Jeff. "Take those classic meetings we have. Ted schedules them for 9 AM sharp and invariably shows up at 9:30 AM, and forbid if there were ever an agenda."

"Yeah, if there were an agenda," agreed Tom, "he wouldn't stick to it anyway. He does all the talking, too. I guess it doesn't matter if we're there or not. It seems our meetings are a real waste of time."

Case Analysis

Listening to Tom and Jeff's conversation, we feel the frustration and sense the disorganization imposed by a manager who unwittingly disrupts his department's work flow and impedes his engineers' productivity. His seeming lack of sensitivity to his people's assignments, deadlines, and personal needs creates barriers to project completion, work quality, and harmonious working relationships.

It is bad enough to constantly disrupt job-related assignments, but unforgivable to interrupt an employee's planned training program, especially for a trivial matter. And as we learned, Tom's program was of particular importance to him and his career—something a manager should instinctively appreciate.

One of the greatest time wasters in business today is poorly planned and conducted meetings. Not only does Ted waste his staff's time by regularly showing up late to meetings, but he also wastes their time by not having an agenda and doing all the talking himself.

An agenda would make his meetings more effective and help control time waste. In addition, meetings requiring no discussion or meetings totally dominated by one speaker might be better handled by way of e-mail or inter-office memos, saving hours and hours each month.

Action Tools

To effectively plan and control your own time and skillfully coordinate departmental activities and work schedules with your staff, consider the following action tools:

- ✸ Once work assignments are determined, help protect your employees' time so that projects can be completed on schedule without unnecessary interruptions.
- ✸ In the event of additional pressing work or necessary job changes, clearly explain the new work to your employees and show flexibility in helping rearrange existing job priorities and schedules.
- ✸ Always consider employee work capacity and avoid dumping new jobs on top of existing assignments, especially when employees are working over capacity.

Such dumping causes employee frustration, reduces job quality, and sets up conditions for not meeting schedules and production deadlines.

* Protect employee professional development activities, such as participation in important courses, seminars, or workshops. These types of assignments are extremely important to employees as well as to the company and clearly communicate management's commitment to employee development. Disruption of such activities risks alienating those you wish to develop into allies and strong team players.

65

Making Timely Decisions

Case Problem: "The Procrastinator"

"Look, the reason I can't stand working with Karl is that he never gets around to making up his mind," said Al, a senior chemist, about his manager. "Procrastination must be his middle name. I could understand once in a while, but he's that way with everything."

"Yes, he is a terrible procrastinator," agreed Kim, a colleague. "If only he would let us make our own decisions concerning the projects we're working on. That would save an enormous amount of time and frustration."

"You're right," agreed Al. "I wish he'd trust us more. I get so upset waiting for him to approve or authorize every little thing. I constantly hear, 'I'll get to it tomorrow.' And, of course, he never does."

"It's true," sighed Kim. "Why, it's been weeks since I first asked Karl about the purchase of the new diagnostic equipment, and he still hasn't made a decision."

"Tell me about it," responded Al. "He also hasn't made a hiring decision about that vacant tech writer's position. The fact is that any of the candidates he has seen would work out just fine. He knows how much we need help in the lab. Why can't he decide? Why doesn't he come to us for our opinions?"

"Since Karl has become manager, we've been in one big holding pattern around here," remarked Kim. "And what can hurt us even more is that the vice president probably thinks that you and I—not Karl—are the causes of major project delays."

Case Analysis

In this case, two scientists are frustrated by their lack of authority in making basic job-related decisions on their own and by their manager's procrastination in making needed departmental decisions.

The manager's failure to empower his scientists with decision-making authority, as well as his tendency to put off important decisions, causes severe productivity and morale problems for his department.

Action Tools

To help move work forward in a timely manner, a manager should delegate as many of the day-to-day job-related decisions as possible to the staff doing the work. For decisions with department-wide impact that should be handled by the manager, the following suggestions should be followed:

* When a decision must be made, first determine its priority and then schedule the date on your calendar for making the decision.
* Review your calendar periodically to make sure that scheduled deadlines are met.
* If decisions can be handled with little work on your part, make them immediately.
* Whenever possible, involve the staff in decisions affecting the whole department.
* Do not avoid needed decisions or place them on the back burner; they will not disappear.

66

Organizing the Office and Work Area

Case Problem: "The Disorganized Organizer"

"John, I can't believe your office. It's such a mess!" said Sam, the accounting manager about one of his accountants' offices. "It's a wonder you can find anything around here. I just hope you can find the report you owe me for today's meeting."

"Oh, yes, the report," replied John, the accountant. "I finished that two days ago, and I know it's around here somewhere."

"See, John," said Sam as he watched John search for the report, "this is what I've been talking about. There's no organization in your office. Your desk looks like a bomb hit it, and there's hardly room to move around in here. It's hard to believe that you've been here for three years. One would think you just came on board and hadn't settled in yet."

"Oh, I just remembered," said John as he suddenly stood up. "Kelly has the report. I gave the rough draft to her on Tuesday for preparation."

Later that day, Sam was discussing his accountants' general lack of organization with his friend, Larry, from the engineering department.

"So, Larry, that's the situation around here. I honestly believe that we lose a lot of valuable time and energy because my accountants apparently have never learned the importance of office organization."

As Sam was conveying his tale of woe, Larry, looking around Sam's office, suddenly spoke up.

"Sam, you've got to be kidding," remarked Larry. "Just look at your own office. It's an absolute mess. Where do you get off criticizing your employees? Look at your shelves. You've got some very pretty knick-knacks on them, but your books and magazines are stacked on the floor against the walls. And look at your files! Shouldn't they be in those cabinets and not spread out all over your desk and chairs?"

"Hold on, friend," replied Sam, defensively. "I don't want put-downs from you. I've come to talk to you about my employees' problems, not mine."

"But that's just it," responded Larry, in a supportive tone. "You have the same problem that you're accusing your people of: disorganization. One way you can help them to improve is to set a positive example yourself."

Case Analysis

Sam's efforts in organizing his own office would provide vivid proof to others of his own interest in and commitment to office organization. In addition, he must provide employees with the necessary organizing resources, including filing cabinets and bookshelves. He must also provide the necessary coaching to help each employee set up and maintain efficient files and office procedures.

Action Tools

Help to organize your department's office and work areas by following these suggestions:

- ✶ Set an example in office and work area organization for your employees by keeping your own area neat and orderly.
- ✶ Provide each employee with adequate filing cabinets and bookshelves as well as other necessary organizing resources and supplies.
- ✶ Help each employee set up and maintain an effective records management procedure.
- ✶ Encourage office and work space organization, and point out the benefits of improved productivity and reduced frustration.

67

Maintaining Self-Control in Stressful Situations

Case Problem: "Hot Under the Collar"

"What is with you, Rita?" asked Karl, vice president of sales and marketing, of his national sales manager. "Can't you ever do anything right? No wonder I'm going crazy checking and rechecking your department's work!"

Just ten minutes earlier, Karl had finished getting chewed out by his boss, the senior vice president. Based on what his boss had said, Karl understood that an important report had been prepared with all the wrong data.

"Look, Rita," continued Karl, "the bottom line is you messed up! Now, who prepared that report? What's the name of the culprit? I'm going to give that person a piece of my mind!"

"Karl, hold on, will you?" interrupted Rita.

"The name!" demanded Karl.

"It's Ebins, the new guy I recently brought on board," explained Rita. "Please let me call him in and find out for myself what happened."

"No way, I'll do it myself," replied Karl. "It seems I have to do everything around here anyway."

While Karl was getting Ebins on the phone, Rita was trying to compose herself. She was totally shocked at Karl's behavior and wanted to resolve the problem herself. After all, Ebins was a member of her staff. Rita could only see her relationship with Ebins being destroyed by Karl's bad temper and interference.

Once on the phone, Karl proceeded to attack Ebins. "You ruined everything; nothing was done right!"

As Karl slammed the phone down, he remarked, "Now let that creep stew for a while!"

Case Analysis

Karl should not have lost his cool. Instead, he should have explained the problem to Rita as it was presented to him and sought her explanation, input, and solutions. It is easy to buckle under to pressure by attacking and condemning others, but keeping one's cool under fire and stress and making an effort to understand a problem require both strength and professionalism.

By his action, Karl, the vice president of sales and marketing, has hurt his credibility, not only with his national sales manager, but with a new employee.

Karl's negative communication with the employee undermined Rita's management authority and hurt her effectiveness in developing her staff.

Action Tools

Consider the following suggestions when under stress:

- Keep your cool in solving a problem, especially when you are under the gun yourself.
- Don't jump to conclusions about an employee's guilt and take disciplinary action without checking out the situation personally.
- Speak to those individuals who are involved in the problem to discover the causes of the problem.

68

Managing Stress

Case Problem: "Keeping Cool"

"I've got a knot in my neck, my eyes are twitching, and I feel like I'm ready to jump out of my skin in this place!" complained Jack, the maintenance superintendent.

As his friend, Mark, the materials manager, listened to his problems, Jack picked up his ringing phone and immediately began berating the caller. After reprimands and threats, Jack slammed down the phone.

"I can't believe the incompetence around here," he complained. "I work hard, sometimes fifteen hours a day, and have to deal with incompetence, crisis after crisis, unrealistic budgets, insane deadlines, and untrained staff. It's just incredible."

"Hold on, Jack," cautioned Mark, trying to calm his friend. "Everything will be all right. What's happening to you?"

"I don't know," replied Jack. "I feel so out of control in this place lately. It seems as though this company is swallowing me up, and I can't seem to get out from under it."

"In what way?" questioned Mark, continuing to listen to his friend in a supportive and sympathetic manner.

Case Analysis

In this case, a stressed-out manager with a deep sense of frustration and powerlessness, appears to be at the mercy of his work environment, allowing people and events to adversely affect his sense of well-being. Fortunately, though, the manager has a sympathetic and supportive friend who cares to listen to his negative feelings.

At times of great stress, such a friend, who can listen well in an empathetic and nonjudgmental manner, is indispensable in helping an individual regain a sense of perspective, reality, and harmony.

Action Tools

A manager has a double role in managing stress at work: first, in the self-control of personal stress, and second, in the management of stress among members of the team.

To help others deal effectively with their stress, you first have to gain control of your own stress by considering the following action tools:

- ✸ View problems as positive opportunities for improvement.
- ✸ Realize that while certain types of problems are not easily handled, many stressful situations are preventable or controllable with proper planning, courage, and perseverance.
- ✸ Practice stress management techniques such as walking, physical workouts, meditation, and outside hobbies and interests.
- ✸ Try to talk out personal problems with trusted friends and advisers in order to obtain a fresh perspective.
- ✸ Involve yourself in social, spiritual, and recreational activities to help rekindle your vital energy. Armed with a positive attitude and an array of personal stress management techniques, you are now prepared to carry out your second stress management role: that of helping manage stress among team members.

To help others deal effectively with their stress, consider the following action tools:

- ✸ Provide time for genuine listening and emotional support.

✱ Bring stressful situations within the department to the team's attention for open and honest team problem-solving.

✱ Confront problems and resolve conflicts among individuals who hinder teamwork and create obstacles to departmental success.

✱ Share with your employees successful stress management approaches that have helped you in your life.

About the Authors

Margaret Mary Gootnick and Dr. David Gootnick are principles with David Gootnick Associates, a New York–based management training and development firm. The firm provides top-rated seminars and workshops on management, team-building, assertiveness, presentation skills, and communication to major corporations throughout America.

Executives and professionals from hundreds of major companies and institutions have attended the courses of David Gootnick Associates. These include Xerox, IBM, TRW, DuPont, Johnson & Johnson, Bethlehem Steel, Procter & Gamble, Milliken & Company, Moore Business Forms, Bristol-Myers Squibb, Metropolitan Life, Federal Express, Citibank, Pasteur Merieux Connaught, Blue Cross/Blue Shield, and The World Bank.

Margaret Mary Gootnick and Dr. David Gootnick are nationally recognized authorities in management, and have written and edited numerous books, journals, and articles, including the popular books *Even You Can Give a Talk, Getting a Better Job,* and *The Standard Handbook of Business Communication.*

Both consultants have served as management instructors for the American Chemical Society, the National Association of Accountants, the American Society of Civil Engineers, and the American Management Association. In addition, they have delivered their popular programs at major universities throughout the nation, including Rensselaer Polytechnic Institute, the State University of New York, the University of Pittsburgh, and Temple University.

Margaret Mary Gootnick has served on the business faculties of New York University's Business Management Institute and Marymount Manhattan College, and has earned the distinction of being listed in *WHO'S WHO of American Women, WHO'S WHO in Professional and Executive Women, International Leaders in Achievement, The International WHO'S WHO of Professional and Business Women*, and *WHO'S WHO in Finance and Industry*.

Index